Cognition and Learning

A Review of the Literature
with
Reference to Ethnolinguistic Minorities

Cognition and Learning

A Review of the Literature
with
Reference to Ethnolinguistic Minorities

Patricia M. Davis

A Publication of

The Summer Institute of Linguistics

1991

Cover design by Hazel Shorey

Copies of this and other publications of the Summer Institute of Linguistics may be obtained from

International Academic Bookstore
Summer Institute of Linguistics
7500 W. Camp Wisdom Road
Dallas, TX 75236

Table of Contents

Preface

This volume is a review of the published literature dealing with cognition and learning, especially as they relate to ethnolinguistic minorities. Chapter one focuses on developmental theories, chapter two reviews information-processing theories, and chapter three treats learning styles, with a special focus on the holistic learner. Following each chapter is a list of references which, though not exhaustive, do bring together under one cover a more comprehensive list than have heretofore been compiled.

A longitudinal study, the book traces the development of present-day thinking. It also contains suggestions for educators facing the challenges of cross-cultural classrooms.

Acknowledgments

I owe a debt of gratitude to Dr. Gary McKenzie of the University of Texas at Austin who allowed me to do chapter one as part of his course work and then graciously took time to provide feedback.

I am deeply grateful to authors Beth Graham, Steven Harris, Judith Lingenfelter, Atilano Valencia, and colleagues of the Summer Institute of Linguistics who consented to my use of long quotes from their works in chapter three.

Gratitude is also due Olive Shell who gave up personal time to read an early draft of the manuscript and to comment; to Manuel Ramiriz III, Dolores Cardenas, and Judith Lingenfelter for their comments; to colleague Diane Cowie for her help on the bibliographical references; and to Steve Walter who went the second mile to provide computer support and who personally facilitated the mechanics of the data processing.

1
Developmental Theories

For centuries, intellectuals have pondered the mysteries of human cognition and have sought to understand how mental development relates to learning ability. Among the studies undertaken in the West during the past hundred years, two aspects of the topic have special relevance for this paper: universal constants and cultural variations. Slowly and haltingly, a body of information has been compiled which enriches our knowledge and has significant application for teachers engaged in cross-cultural education. This chapter reviews developmental theories reported in the literature.

1.1 Genetic programming

Early studies, for our purposes, began with the American psychologists James Mark Baldwin and G. Stanley Hall. Baldwin proposed a theory that described children's development as going through stages, which he identified in terms of "circular reactions", "accommodation," and "adaptation" (Baldwin 1894; Dworetzky 1987:226). Hall postulated that the human brain evolves through stages because of genetic programming (1917:1-6, 234-37; 1920: vii-xviii, 449-54). The stages are:

> The *Simian* stage, in which the subject cannot understand abstract ideas but learns by reward and punishment.

> The *Savage* stage, in which the subject cannot understand abstract ideas but learns through modelling.

> The *Rational* stage, in which the subject can understand abstract ideas and is able to learn through discovery.

Hall directed his research towards common experience (e.g., 'What are clouds?') rather than academic knowledge. However, he felt that mental development could be hindered if pushed prematurely so recommended that teachers not present powerful ideas until students had reached adolescence. By then, according to Hall's theory, genes and natural instinct would automatically have developed more advanced reasoning powers. These views coincided with Darwinian teachings concerning physical and social evolution.

The theories of genetic programming and social evolution received considerable attention with the discovery of the Australian Aborigines. Seizing the opportunity for cross-cultural research, an expedition set out to the Torres Straits (Rivers 1901). There the Aborigines' "lack of material possessions, instead of being viewed as the purposeful and successful product of efficient adaptation by hunter-gatherers, was rather interpreted as a sign of cultural impoverishment, with its inevitable concomitant of intellectual inferiority" (Klich and Davidson 1984:157).

It seemed to make no difference that Rivers' testing of Aborigines in 1901 had, in some cases, produced results higher than those of the islanders of non-Aboriginal descent, that other researchers had observed unusual Aboriginal competence in hunting and tracking (Klich and Davidson 1984:158–59), or that Levi Strauss had stated that in relation to family organization the Aboriginals were "so far ahead of the rest of mankind that, to understand the careful and deliberate systems of rules they have elaborated, we have to use all the refinements of modern mathematics" (cited in Franklin 1976:9). Consistent with Hall's theory, it was thought probable that intellectual development in the Aboriginal was permanently stunted. "The predominate attention of the savage to concrete things around him may act as an obstacle to higher mental development" (Rivers 1901:45). Porteus speculated that Aborigines probably suffered from "a slower rate of development through the whole growing period, or what is more likely, an earlier cessation of brain growth than is observable in Europeans" (1933:32).

These conclusions appear unjustified in view of the results of some of Porteus' own tests in which certain Aborigines equalled their Western peers (1931:401). However, Porteus concluded that "a so-called primitive race such as the Australians may be excellently adapted to their own environment and therefore must be deemed intelligent. But at the same time they are certainly unadaptable to a civilized environment" (1931:376).

1.2 Piagetian theory

Seeking more precise information concerning non-Western minority societies, researchers began to orient their investigations in terms of Jean Piaget's model of cognitive development. Piaget was a brilliant Swiss scholar who, at the age of twenty-two had earned a Ph.D. in natural science (zoology) and by age thirty had published about twenty-five papers on mollusks and related topics (Lefrancois 1988:180). He also studied psychology, psychopathy, logic, and epistemology (the study of the nature of knowledge).

In 1920, he found himself at Binet's laboratory school in Paris, undertaking to standardize some mental tests in connection with Theodore Simon, a codeveloper with Alfred Binet of a children's intelligence test. In his approach to the task, Piaget was influenced by the writings of Baldwin and his training in biological observation and description (Dworetzky 1981). He became fascinated with his discovery that children the same age often gave the same incorrect answers to questions, and he set about to investigate the manner in which children's thinking processes develop, and in what ways they perceive the world differently at different points of the process. Underlying his research were two unifying questions: (1) What characteristics enable children to adapt to their environment? and (2) What is the most simple, accurate, and useful way to classify child development? (Lefrancois 1988:180). Piaget understood all human development in terms of adaptation to the environment. For him, adaptation was made possible through assimilation (using a response already acquired) or through accommodation (modifying a response to meet the new need).

Since the goal was to find universal developmental principles, Piaget's research focussed on common experience, not academic knowledge, which might act as a skewing factor. His questioning took the form of interviews about things in the real world. Eventually, he proposed a multi-faceted theory of great breadth which deals with intelligence and perception (Piaget 1972a; Hunt 1961; Seagrim and Lendon 1980), and which is difficult to summarize without falling into distortion, oversimplification, or misrepresentation (Flavell 1977:6). It related his concept of intelligence as a product of biological adaptation to theoretical issues in epistemology and was unique in the literature of the day.

Piaget's contributions—according to the Academic American Encyclopedia (1986:287–88)—fall into four main areas: the general stages of intellectual development from infancy through adulthood (e.g., Ginsburg and Opper 1979); studies of perceptual development (e.g., Piaget 1976); how children come to understand scientific concepts such as time and space (e.g., Piaget 1954); and questions of theoretical epistemology (e.g., Piaget

1971). In the process, he dealt with most facets of human functioning—language (1926), causality (1930), time (1946a), velocity (1946b), movement (1946b), judgment and reasoning (1928), logic (1957b), number (1952; Piaget et al. 1981), play (1951), imitation (1951), and physics (1957a)—(Lefrancois 1988:179).

Piaget's own works are weighty; reviews by other authors such as Ginsburg and Opper (1979) are easier to read. However, although Piaget began as a biologist and naturalist, his writings (over fifty books) have profoundly affected the field of contemporary developmental psychology, and he has been named by Lefrancois as "the most prolific and influential child development researcher in the world" (1988:180).

Piaget is best known for classifying four stages of human cognitive development, with much elaboration and many subdivisions. A brief summary follows:

1. The *Sensorimotor* stage (0–2 years) in which learning is perceived as expanding perceptual and musculature systems. The main subdivisions within this stage are:

   Stage 1 (0–1 month):   reflex activity
   Stage 2 (1–4 months):   self-investigation
   Stage 3 (4–8 months):   coordination and reaching out
   Stage 4 (8–12 months):   goal-directed behavior
   Stage 5 (12–18 months):   experimentation
   Stage 6 (18–24 months):   mental combinations and problem solving

2. The *Preoperational* stage (2–7 years) in which learning is said to take place through experimentation. The main divisions in this period are:

   The *Preconceptual* stage (2–4 years): emergence of symbolic functions, syncretic and transductive reasoning, and animism.

   The *Intuitive* stage (4–7 years): the child centers on one aspect at a time; egocentrism.

3. The *Concrete Operational* stage (7–11 years) in which understanding is tied to experience but some internal symbolism begins to be used. Here logical operations are applied to concrete problems, and numbers can be understood. Conservation of number, length, mass, area, and volume are now obtained, as well as reversibility, seriation, and classification skills.

4. The *Formal Operations* stage (12 years and on) in which learning is highly internal, symbolic, and relatively free of direct experience, such that hypothetical reasoning becomes possible, including generalization, idealism, and ethical reasoning. In this stage subjects can solve hypothetical problems, make complex deductions, and test advanced hypotheses. They can also analyze the validity of different ways of reasoning—the foundation of scientific investigation.

(Piaget 1972b, 1932; Dworetzky 1987:228; Lefrancois 1988:184–95).

Piaget's descriptions of young children's intellectual maturation processes are important for mothers and educators. This paper, however, focuses on stages three and four, the stages applicable to school-age children. Facility in formal operations is extremely important for learning in Western-oriented school systems.

Piagetian theory differed from Hall's genetic programming in that Piaget argued that children assimilate information into an existing *cognitive structure* until a point at which the concept is so well established that it allows new forms of reasoning. Thought, therefore, was attributed to knowledge, not to genetics. Intelligence was considered to be an everchanging process of interaction with and adaptation to the environment. Intellectual development results in changes in behavior (Lefrancois 1988:182). The term cognitive structure was used as a metaphor to denote the qualities of intellect which govern behavior (Lefrancois 1988:183).

As early as 1966, Piaget (1974) had discussed the need for cross-cultural research in genetic psychology, and it was thought useful to ascertain whether the same stages of development observed in Western societies would be evident among ethnolinguistic minorities. The following are examples of studies which were carried out to test for the stages of concrete and formal operations, the two stages which are relevant to educational endeavors.

The concrete operational stage

Between 1959 and 1969 a number of studies focussed upon the skills involved in a subject's ability to conserve weight and measure despite variations in the shape and size of the mass. Seven of the more well-known are listed by Heron and Simonsson (1974:335) as follows: Aden: Hyde, 1959; Nigeria: Price-Williams, 1961; Hong Kong: Goodnow, 1962; Senegal: Greenfield, 1966; Australian Aborigines: de Lemos, 1969; Papua New Guinea: Prince, 1968; Jamaica, Canadian Esquimaux and Indians: Vernon, 1969.

The concept of conservation (tested by pouring water into different shaped containers, or moulding the same ball of clay into different shapes) aroused interest because of its proximity to formal operations, the highest level of cognitive development in Piaget's scheme. The results of the studies varied widely, and several of these investigators expressed concern as to the validity of their findings, conscious that unanticipated cultural variables might be influencing results. Greenfield and Bruner (1966:94), for example, reported that it was necessary for Wolof children of Senegal to pour the water themselves in order to eliminate suspicion of a "magical" explanation for the seeming inequality of the water in their beakers.

In research of a different nature, de Lacey, reporting on a study first published in 1970, sought to ascertain whether classificatory ability was related to environment by contrasting Australian Aboriginal children with Australian children of European descent. Among the Aboriginals there was "consistent and strong direct relationship between classificatory performance and the degree of contact with Europeans and their technology" (1974:363).

Subjects who evidenced a middle range of cognitive skills were reported by Bovet (1974:313–34). Bovet hypothesized that cognitive reasoning would reach higher levels for concepts linked to oft-repeated activities and might—contrary to the beliefs of some—even reach the level of formal operations. Her tests, conducted in Arabic with unschooled Algerian children ages six to thirteen and illiterate adults thirty-five to fifty years of age, measured conservation of quantity with liquids and plasticine, conservation of weight with clay balls, and conservation of spatial relations (length) with sticks.

When the Algerian group was compared with a control group of children from Geneva, a difference became apparent in the order in which conservation concepts were acquired.

Geneva		Algeria	
Conservation of quantity	Conservation of weight + length	Conservation of quantity + length	Conservation of weight
7–8 years	9 years	9 years	12–13 years

Illiterate adults in Algeria, presented with the same tasks as the children, evidenced no difficulty with concepts of liquid conservation, but women used to estimating the weight of bread dough by testing it in their hands had difficulty judging the weight of objects by looking at them.

Commenting upon the results, Bovet notes the influence of environmental conditioning (there were no standard-sized vessels in the culture), and concluded in answer to her initial question that higher levels of cognition are indeed demonstrable for activities which take place frequently.

The formal operations stage

Despite these observations, lively discussion continued as to whether technologically undeveloped peoples could reach the stage of abstract reasoning. In New Guinea, working with verbal logical and empirical formal tests, Were failed to find any trace of formal thought among fourteen to sixteen year olds (1968, reported in Dasen 1974:412). Lancy states that in New Guinea "not one society has games with elements that would seem to tax higher-order problem-solving or memory skills" (1983:119, quoting Townshend 1979). Lancy concluded as regards New Guinean systems of classification, "While there are categories, these are not mutually exclusive: They are not nested in a hierarchy and the mention of a category name creates no press to list exemplars of a category" (1983:116). Wilson and Wilson, after testing over five hundred pre-tertiary students in Papua New Guinea, concluded that "at the beginning of Grade 11, very few students are at the stage of early, still less late, formal operational thought" (1983:8). Approximately a quarter of each group tested, however, were at a "transitional level" and so were able to perform formal operations in some situations.

This finding is low compared with thirty percent of sixteen-year olds in the United States, who attain formal operations before leaving school (Shayer, Adey, and Wylam 1981). The Papua New Guinea subjects, however, made significant gains in cognitive level in the following year or two while studying college preparatory courses (Wilson and Wilson 1983:9). Wilson and Wilson conclude that although "the early traditional environment of Papua New Guinea students does not stimulate optimum cognitive development in Piagetian terms, there is certainly evidence of significant development . . . indicating that early disadvantages can be overcome." Confirming evidence is provided by Seagrim and Lendon (1980:181), who—after an extensive study—concluded that Australian Aboriginal children are capable of matching white children in all of the Piagetian thought forms after a period of total immersion in white culture. Those remaining in Aboriginal culture lag far behind.

In summary, studies which compare educated and noneducated subjects, consistently show earlier or more rapid development of cognitive abilities in the more educated group.

1.3 Applications in western society

Piaget's concept of sequential stages of cognitive development has been enormously useful to psychologists, educators, and parents. His theory is included in textbooks for teacher-training (e.g., Reilly and Lewis 1983; Gallahue, Werner and Luedke 1975; Dworetzky 1987; Ginsburg and Opper 1979; Lefrancois 1988), and is a major criterion used to evaluate the adequacy of teaching materials for all grade levels. Since Piaget's writings stimulated many other studies, not all of which confirmed his findings, the literature reads much like a dialogue between Piaget and his fellow researchers. He constantly revised and expanded his theory as new information came to light. For example, after 1932 he admitted the need "to compare the behavior of children of different social backgrounds to be able to distinguish the social from the individual in their thinking" (Vygotsky 1962:9).

Later interchanges between Piaget and the great Russian psychologist L. S. Vygotsky contributed towards Piaget's reformulating his statements to include language development as an essential step in symbolizing actions abstractly (Vygotsky 1962:vii, 9–24; Piaget 1962). He also recognized that stimulating environments tend to speed the age at which a child reaches the ability to think with formal operations processes (Piaget 1972a:6–8; Hunt 1961:346–47, 362–63).

In his 1972 writings Piaget also allowed for different rates of progression through the stages of development, especially from one culture to another, recognizing that "children often vary in terms of the areas of functioning to which they apply formal operations, according to their aptitudes and professional specializations" (1972a:1; see also Inhelder, Sinclair and Bovet 1974:128). In these respects, Piaget differs from earlier developmentalists, who ascribed less importance to socialization and to educational transmission.

Examples of studies which have continued to expand on and challenge Piaget's conclusions are as follows.

Hatch observed that young children often demonstrate metalinguistic awareness and by age five or six can abstract rules in second language situations (1978:14–15).

Donaldson found that even young children can use abstract thought, although not in the exact format prescribed by Piaget (1978:56–59).

Desforges and Brown quote studies in which even Western postgraduate students failed tests of conservation and conclude that Piagetian stages are "only tangential to the main educational issue, which is why children fail with certain materials and succeed with others" (1979:279).

Entwistle, citing the above studies, comments that Piagetian-type tests favor scientific thinkers and do not allow for intuitive thought. He also feels that although prerequisite cognitive skills may account for nonuse of formal operations in some students, this lack may not indicate a deficiency in such abilities but rather "lack of previous knowledge or experience, or . . . a low level of interest in the task presented or content area being studied" (1981:173).

To this Christie (1982) and Graham (1986) would add lack of understanding of the purposes of schooling and the processes involved as well as inability to manipulate language genres as skillfully as is necessary in the classroom.

One must also question whether cognitive processes (such as conservation), which normally develop through increased life experience, should be equated with, or serve as indicators of, capability in academic reasoning, which is not normally learned through life experience but rather must be taught.

1.4 Applications in ethnolinguistic minority groups

Studies which have attempted to apply Piagetian theory cross-culturally have encountered numerous problems, in large part due to unconscious biases and lack of cultural orientation on the part of the researchers which have resulted in inappropriate evaluation instruments. McLaughlin (1976:87–90) ennumerates problems which have characterized cross-cultural studies in Africa. Among them: elusive variables, cultural factors which require special skills to interpret, and problems in making fair and equal comparisons between cultures. McLaughlin asserts that all subjects show higher-level cognitive processes but differ in the range of situations to which they apply.

Klich and Davidson listed their concerns in relation to the many studies carried out in Australia. These concerns are valid for any cross-cultural testing.

- Language barriers. (Most of the tests were administered in English to subjects whose English competence was limited and whose language forms did not equate certain abstract terms used in the testing.)

- Testing through performance tasks rather than through Piagetian interviews.

- The hazards implicit when subjects in one culture are required to respond to stimuli and procedures designed by researchers from another culture. This includes unfamiliar testing situations.

- Uncertainty as to whether the Piagetian model is universal.

- The assumption that cognitive competence in white culture and cognitive competence in Aboriginal culture are mutually exclusive.
(1984:169–71)

Seeking to identify the abstract functions behind culturally different modes of organizing information, Klich and Davidson (1984:182) availed themselves of the neuropsychological work of A. R. Luria (1966), who considered higher mental functions to be "complex, organized functional systems that operate as the result of interactions between differentiated brain structures." They designed a study the results of which indicated that "no apparent difference in the underlying pattern of cognitive processing functions between these samples of Aboriginal and non-Aboriginal children could be established" on the eleven tests administered (1984:164).

Klich and Davidson's rigorous and culturally oriented testing procedures included: instructions in the vernacular language; administration of tests by the regular Aboriginal teacher either to groups, or within sight and hearing of other Aboriginals; practice items to assure comprehension of each procedure; and opportunity for the child to nominate the next person to take the test (all accommodations to Aboriginal orientation). These factors, combined with test refinements incorporated as the result of previous studies, auger well for the reliability of the Klich and Davidson test results and serve as a model for future investigators.

More recently, studies have focussed on memory skills, visual memory, route-finding skills, card playing, and temporal and spatial ordering, which have been recognized as decidedly superior in Australian Aboriginals in comparison to Europeans (Klich and Davidson 1984:172–76), but are not arrived at by the mental processes a Westerner would expect.

1.5 Successive equilibration

In 1974, Piaget expanded his theory, stating that four main factors interact to promote a child's ability to think with increasing complexity: (1) maturation, (2) equilibration, i.e., auto regulation, (3) general socialization, and (4) educational and cultural transmission (1974:300–303).

Voyat (1983:131), who conducted extensive studies with seventy-one Sioux children ages four through ten, found all four stages developing in the sequences predicted by Piaget. He also found maturation to be a less influential factor in cognitive development than experience coupled with dynamic deduction: "Neither Oglala nor Geneva children have an intuition of conservation or space; they build it" (1983:134). He distinguishes between physical experiences which lead to direct abstraction from the object, and logico-mathematical experiences which refer to the result of actions. Logico-mathematical knowledge is acquired through successive equilibration rather than through additive knowledge. Because "many discoveries that a child makes during his life are not due to educative or social transmissions," Voyat (1983:134–35) feels that equilibration (assimilation of information and its accommodation within mental structures already present) is the key mechanism of cognitive development and organizational learning.

The equilibration theory may help to explain why adults in minority societies may not be able to perform Western-type conservation activities but do evidence other types of abstract reasoning. One example is the complex calculations used in mathematical games such as *mankala*, which are played in many non-Western cultures and existed long before the advent of the white man (Townshend 1979:794).

1.6 Educational implications

Given all of the above, one question has continued to haunt educators: Since members of nontechnological societies are capable of abstraction and hypothetical reasoning, why do numbers of them experience extreme difficulty in Western-type school settings. (The Australian Aborigines are but one example.)

Malone feels that most illiterate minority societies are illiterate because for them literacy is not necessary. Testing for cognitive development "may be relevant for testing Western scientific acculturation, not for testing basic psychological processes" (1985:38). Malone cites studies which have found that African students performed better when tests were adjusted to culturally relevant and ecologically valid inference habits: Cole et al. 1971; Ross and Millsom 1970; Segall et al. 1966; Pollack 1963; Berry 1971; Jahoda 1971.

Geoffrey Hunt (1989:425) postulates that hunting and gathering cultures, with numbering systems that distinguish only between one and many, and language systems which have few, if any, logical connectives and perhaps few abstract expressions (e.g., anyone, someone) have practically no need for abstraction. Instead, concepts and language develop in other areas such as spatial relationships, in which Aborigines far outstrip Europeans. Until abstraction skills are developed, however, many of the concepts taught in Western schools will be very difficult for aboriginal people to learn, especially if the student remains in an environment where there is no practical need for abstraction.

Modern consensus now recognizes environmental, familial, and societal factors to be prime elements in cognitive development, along with normal maturation processes, language development, and educational opportunity.

1.7 Conclusion

Developmental theory was proposed by James Mark Baldwin and expanded by G. Stanley Hall, who postulated that the human brain evolves through stages as a result of genetic programming. Jean Piaget subsequently studied and described the processes of intellectual development and is best known for his classification of four stages: the sensorimotor stage, the preoperational stage, the concrete operational stage, and the formal operations stage.

Piaget also studied perceptual development, and how children come to understand scientific concepts. He related these questions to theoretical epistemology. Later in his career, Piaget realized that individuals may progress at different rates as they advance through the stages of development. Differences in the rate of progression between individuals of different cultures are especially noticeable. Piaget also advanced the theory of successive equilibration, holding that maturation, auto regulation, general socialization, and educational and cultural transmission enhance a child's ability to think with increasing complexity. He further recognized the importance of language development, which is an essential step towards abstract symbolization, a skill necessary to be able to think with formal operations processes.

Piaget is rightly respected for his contributions to developmental psychology. Although he died before he could give attention to the processes involved in academic learning, he paved the way for today's thinking that learned knowledge enables mental development and abstract thought.

References

Academic American Encyclopedia. 1986. Danbury, Connecticut: Grolier, Inc.

Baldwin, J. M. 1894. The development of the child and of the race. New York: McMillan.

Berry, J. W. 1971. Muller-Lyer susceptibility: culture, ecology or race? International Journal of Psychology 6:193–97.

Bovet, M. C. 1974. Cognitive processes among illiterate children and adults. In J. W. Berry and P. R. Dasen (eds.), Culture and cognition: readings in cross-cultural psychology, 311–34. London: Methuen.

Christie, Michael. 1982. The ritual reader: guiding principles for teaching meaningful reading to Aboriginal children. Paper presented at the Eighth Australian Reading Conference, Adelaide, Australia.

Cole, M., J. Gay, J. Glick, and D. Sharp. 1971. The cultural context of learning and thinking. New York: Basic Books.

Dasen, P. R. 1974. Cross-cultural Piagetian research: A summary. In J. W. Berry and P. R. Dasen (eds.), Culture and cognition: readings in cross-cultural psychology, 409–23. London: Methuen.

de Lacey, P. R. 1974. A cross-cultural study of classificatory ability in Australia. In J. W. Berry and P. R. Dasen (eds.), Culture and cognition: readings in cross-cultural psychology, 353–65. London: Methuen.

de Lemos, M. M. 1969. The development of conservation in Aboriginal children. International Journal of Psychology 4(4):225–69.

Desforges, C. and G. Brown. 1979. The educational utility of Piaget: a reply to Shayer. British Journal of Educational Psychology 49(3):277–81.

Donaldson, M. 1978. Children's minds. London: Fontana.

Dworetzky, John P. 1987. Introduction to child development. St. Paul, Minnesota: West Publishing Company.

Entwistle, Noel. 1981. Styles of learning and teaching: an integrated outline of educational psychology for students, teachers, and lecturers. Chichester, New York: John Wiley and Sons.

Flavell, John H. 1977. Cognitive development. Englewood Cliffs, New Jersey: Prentice-Hall.

Franklin, M. A. 1976. Black and white Australians. Australia: Heinemann.

Gallahue, David L., Peter H. Werner, and George C. Luedke. 1975. A conceptual approach to moving and learning. New York: John Wiley and Sons.

Ginsburg, Herbert and Sylvia Opper. 1979. Piaget's theory of intellectual development. Englewood Cliffs, New Jersey: Prentice-Hall.

Graham, Beth. 1986. Learning the language of schooling: considerations and concerns in the Aboriginal context. Paper presented at the Australia and New Zealand Conference on the First Years of School, May 12–15, 1986, Sydney, Australia.

Greenfield, Patricia Marks and Jerome S. Bruner. 1966. Culture and cognitive growth. International Journal of Psychology 1(2):89–107.

Hall, G. Stanley. 1917. Youth: its education, regimen and hygiene. New York: D. Appleton and Company.

———. 1920. Adolescence. Vols. 1 and 2. New York: D. Appleton and Company.

Hatch, Evelyn Marcussen. 1978. Second language acquisition: a book of readings. Rowley, Massachusetts: Newbury House.

Heron, A. and M. Simonsson. 1974. Weight conservation in Zambian children: a nonverbal approach. In J. W. Berry and P. R. Dasen (eds.), Culture and cognition: readings in cross-cultural psychology, 335–50. London: Methuen.

Hunt, Geoffrey. 1989. My logic doesn't match yours: limits to translation imposed by cognitive development. Notes on Linguistics 47:4–25. Dallas: Summer Institute of Linguistics.

Hunt, Joseph McVickers. 1961. Intelligence and experience. New York: The Ronald Press Company.

Inhelder, Barbel, Hermine Sinclair, and Magali Bovet. 1974. Learning and the development of cognition. Cambridge, Massachusetts: Harvard University Press.

Jahoda, G. 1971. Retinal pigmentation, illusion susceptibility and space perception. International Journal of Psychology 6:199–208.

Klich, L. Z. and Graham R. Davidson. 1984. Toward a recognition of Australian Aboriginal competence in cognitive functions. In John R. Kirby (ed.), Cognitive strategies and educational performance, 155–202. Orlando, Florida: Academic Press.

Lancy, David F. 1983. Cross-cultural studies in cognition and mathematics. New York: Academic Press.

Lefrancois, Guy R. 1988. Psychology for teaching. Belmont, California: Wadsworth Publishing Company.

Luria, A. R. 1966. Higher cortical functions in man. New York: Basic Books.

Malone, Mike. 1985. Analysis of differences in cognitive development in selected African and Western societies. Anthropology and Appropriate Education 31:35–97.

McLaughlin, S. O. 1976. Cognitive processes and school learning: a review of research on cognition in Africa. African Studies Review 19(1):75–93.

Piaget, Jean. 1926. The language and thought of the child. New York: Harcourt, Brace and World.

———. 1928. Judgment and reasoning in the child. New York: Harcourt, Brace and World.

———. 1930. The child's conception of physical causality. London: Kegan Paul.

———. 1932. The moral judgment of the child. London: Kegan Paul.

———. 1946a. Le developpement de la notion de temps chez l'enfant. Paris: Presses Université France.

———. 1946b. Les notions de mouvement et de vitesse chez l'enfant. Paris: Presses Université France.

———. 1951. Play, dreams and imitation in childhood. New York: W. W. Norton and Company.

———. 1952. The child's conception of number. New York: Humanities Press.

———. 1954. The construction of reality in the child. New York: Basic Books.

———. 1957a. The child and modern physics. Scientific American 196:46–51.

———. 1957b. Logic and psychology. New York: Basic Books.

———. 1962. Comments on Vygotsky's critical remarks. Cambridge, Massachusetts: The M.I.T. Press.

———. 1971. Psychology and epistemology. Kingsport, Tennessee: Kingsport Press.

———. 1972a. Intellectual evolution from adolescence to adulthood. Human Development 15:1–12.

———. 1972b. Science of education and the psychology of the child. New York: Viking Press.

———. 1974. Need and significance of cross-cultural studies in genetic psychology. In J. W. Berry and P. R. Dasen (eds.), Culture and cognition: readings in cross-cultural psychology, 299–309. London: Methuen.

———. 1976. The child's conception of the world. Totowa, New Jersey: Littlefield, Adams and Company.

———, Barbel Inhelder, and Alina Szeminska. 1981. The child's conception of geometry. New York: W.W. Norton and Company.

Pollack, R. H. 1963. Contour detectability thresholds as a function of chronological age. Perceptual and Motor Skills 17:411–17.

Porteus, Stanley D. 1931. The psychology of a primitive people. London: Edward Arnold.

———. 1933. Mentality of Australian Aborigines. Oceania 4:30–36.

Reilly, Robert R. and Ernest L. Lewis. 1983. Jean Piaget: a view of cognitive development. In Educational Psychology: Applications for Classroom Learning and Instruction, 55–89. New York: Macmillan.

Rivers, W. H. R. 1901. Reports of the Cambridge anthropological expedition to the Torres Strait II. Physiology and Psychology. London: Cambridge University Press.

Ross, B. M. and C. Millsom. 1970. Repeated memory of oral prose in Ghana and New York. International Journal of Psychology 5(3):173–81.

Seagrim, Gavin and Robin Lendon. 1980. Furnishing the mind: a comparative study of cognitive development in central Australian Aborigines. New York: Academic Press.

Segall, M. H., D. T. Campbell, and M. J. Herskovits. 1966. The influence of culture on visual perception. New York: Bobbs-Merrill.

Shayer, M., P. Adey and H. Wylam. 1981. Group tests of cognitive development: ideals and a realization. Journal of Research in Science Teaching 18(2):157–58.

Townshend, P. 1979. African *mankala* in anthropological perspective. Current Anthropology 20:794–96.

Voyat, Gilbert. 1983. Cognitive development among Sioux children. New York: Plenum Press.

Vygotsky, L. S. 1962. Thought and language. Cambridge, Massachusetts: The M.I.T. Press.

Were, K. 1968. A survey of the thought processes of New Guinean secondary students. M.Ed. thesis, University of Adelaide, Australia.

Wilson, Audrey and Michael Wilson. 1983. Formal thought among pre-tertiary students in PNG. Papua New Guinea Journal of Education 19(2):1–11.

2

Information Processing Theories

Parallel with the studies carried out in Piagetian tradition, a group of researchers began in the 1960s to direct their attention to the processes involved in academic learning. Especially in focus was the way in which formal instruction can produce learning with effects similar to those of the naturally-developed concepts studied by Piaget. The theories which resulted have not been seriously tested in cross-cultural situations, insofar as I have been able to ascertain; however, the nature of the observations appears to be universal. For that reason, and because they contain concepts useful for teachers in minority societies, they are reviewed in this chapter.

2.1.Reception learning

David P. Ausubel, well-known psychiatrist and professor of medical students, focussed his considerable skill on the cognitive processes involved in adult learning of meaningful verbal material. He espoused expository teaching, which he called reception learning, considering it to be a quicker and more effective method than discovery learning for communicating large quantities of material (1963:19). Ausubel's terminology is somewhat complicated, but the main tenets of his theory are found in numerous books and articles (for example, Ausubel 1963 and 1967; Ausubel, Novak, and Hanesian 1978). A brief summary follows.

People want to learn. Intrinsic motivation impels them to explore knowledge and rewards them with internal satisfaction when they succeed. This *cognitive drive*, as Ausubel terms it, is accommodated by the human mind, which has marvellous capacity for categorization and organization. As

17

information is presented to it, the mind establishes categories and organizes them in hierarchical fashion, from the most general to the most specific.

Learning consists of assigning a concept a place in the cognitive structure and then building more information around it. There can be no learning, however, without meaning. Meaningful learning occurs when students connect a new concept with a network of related concepts already stored in the mind. Sets of linked concepts are called *cognitive structures*.

Intelligence is measured by the number of concepts possessed and the efficiency with which cognitive relationships are organized. The more concepts one has stored in one's mind, the more one is able to learn because there are more categories to which to anchor incoming information.

The teacher is a subject matter expert. He first assesses the domain and chooses from it the portion which he will teach. Second, he identifies the concepts implicit in the chosen material. Third, he analyzes the student (each one individually) to determine what each knows about the subject. If the student already grasps the concepts, the teacher alerts him as to the set he needs to profit from the lesson. If the student does not know the concepts, the teacher has two choices:

1. To create a comparative advance organizer, relating the new concept to something already known.

2. To create an expository advance organizer—a verbal explanation of the main features of the concept—in order to establish it as a category in the student's cognitive structure.

A concept about which the student knows nothing will be a new category. If there is no other concept to which it can be related, the student will have to assign it an arbitrary place in the cognitive structure and learn it by rote. Mastery of rote knowledge is significantly more difficult and time-consuming for students since there is nothing to which to anchor the information until a network of links is established. Ausubel sought always to avoid rote learning by preparing the students with advance organizers.

Not until the teacher is assured that the student understands the concept in the same way as the teacher does, and that they both have the same concept in focus, can the lesson proceed.

When the lesson does go forward, storage of new material in the cognitive structure is called *subsumption*. The category under which details are assimilated is termed the *subsumer*. If the information fits into the category perfectly, the process of accommodation is called *derivative subsumption*. If the category must be extended somewhat to accommodate the new knowledge, the process is called *correlative subsumption*. An item of knowledge subsumed under a main category, may, in turn, have other items subsumed under it, just as a file drawer has main sections and subdivisions, with folders under each. The process of organizing information and anchoring it to appropriate categories is named *integrative reconciliation* (Ausubel 1963:53, 77–78).

Ausubel explained the process of information retrieval by postulating that when data is required (as, for example, for an exam question), a search goes on within the brain. The wanted item is located, dissociated (freed) from the surrounding cognitive structure in which it has been embedded, raised to the threshold of availability, and put into working memory. At times, however, information is so tightly embedded within a larger network that it cannot be dissociated as a discrete item or raised to the threshold of availability. When this occurs, we say the item has been forgotten; Ausubel calls it *obliterative subsumption* (1963:25–26).

Ausubel's theory contains several helps for educators. Building on Piagetian theory, he conceded that "learners who have not yet developed beyond the concrete stage of cognitive development are unable meaningfully to incorporate within their cognitive structures a relationship between two or more abstractions unless they have the benefit of current or recently prior concrete-empirical experience" (1967:19). However, he felt that by junior-high-school level students could grasp higher-order relationships between abstractions, particularly if aided by "proper" expository teaching (1967:19). Since Ausubel's concern was adult medical students, who were well able to reason abstractly, he left the matter there.

Understanding the importance of prior knowledge in achieving understanding and the need, even for adults, to have a knowledge base appropriate to the lesson, enables teachers to facilitate student learning. To this end, Ausubel stressed the need for advance organizers to help students locate and then store new ideas within their cognitive structure. He recommended that advance organizers should:

1. Be presented at a higher level of abstraction than the new material to be learned.
2. Be constructed with the more inclusive concepts presented first and progressively differentiated.
3. Delineate clearly the similarities and differences between the new material and what is already known.
4. Relate new material to established ideas.

(1967:81–83)

Ausubel (1967:83) identified two types of organizer:

> *Comparative* organizers, which use an example to explain the new concept in terms of something already understood. This type is especially useful in cases where students may not realize that they possess information relevant to the subject. (See Appendix A for an example.)

> *Expository* organizers, which use an explanation to identify the essential elements of the new concept. The concept will then serve as a subsumer for the details which will be presented later in the body of the lesson.

Ausubel's ideal was that advance organizers should be constructed for each student and that they should exactly match the individual's knowledge, or lack thereof. Teachers in large classes, however, will have to make educated guesses, or devise ways to determine quickly what the majority of the class knows in relation to a topic, since individual pretesting and preteaching are not possible.

In remediation, and individual tutoring, pretesting and use of advance organizers can enable a teacher to correct previously unidentified misconceptions. Advance organizers are particularly important in cross-cultural education because students may not have categories for the information they are required to learn. Ausubel provides the teacher a way to focus on the new concept and give the student the information he or she needs to build a category for it.

2.2 Schema theory

Schema theory, developed by the respected educational psychologist R. C. Anderson (see Anderson 1977 and 1978; Schallert 1982), views organized knowledge as an elaborate network of schemata—abstract mental structures which represent one's understanding of the world. The term *schema* was brought into modern educational psychology by Piaget in 1926 and is also found in the writings of Wertheimer, Bartlett, and Bruner (Anderson 1978:67; 1977:417). Anderson found this concept of mental processes particularly insightful. He adopted Piaget's term *assimilation* for schema usage and *accommodation* for schema change, but has expanded upon the original meaning of schema in his theory.

A schema, as understood in schema theory, represents generic knowledge. A general category (schema) will include slots for all the components, or features, included in it. Schemata are embedded one within another at different levels of abstraction. Relationships among them are conceived as webs (rather than hierarchies); thus each one is interconnected with many others. For example, a person's schema of 'egg' might include the components shown in the egg diagram below.

Schemata are always organized meaningfully, can be added to, and—as an individual gains experience—develop to include more variables and more specificity. Some variables are obligatory; others are not. Each schema is embedded in other schemata and itself contains subschema. Schemata change moment by moment as information is received. They may also be reorganized when incoming data reveals a need to restructure the concept. The mental representations used during perception and comprehension, and which evolve as a result of these processes, combine to form a whole which is greater than the sum of its parts (Anderson 1977:418–19).

Richards considers that children:

1. Show a definite progression in their acquisition of metaknowledge (awareness of what they personally know, knowledge concerning strategies for learning, etc.).

2. Demonstrate an understanding of the structure of stories between the ages of five and seven years. (Complexity of elaboration increases thereafter.)

3. Move toward greater specificity (narrowing concepts originally understood too broadly) and elaboration (amplifying concepts originally understood too narrowly).

(Schallert 1982:24–25).

Studies involving adults have mostly involved testing which required the subjects to utilize already established schemata in the assimilation of new information. Schallert, a disciple of Richards, quotes studies indicating that abstract concepts are best understood after a foundation of concrete, relevant information has been established (1982:26). The general knowledge provides a framework into which the newly-formed structure can be fitted.

In the interpretation of messages, comprehension develops as the mind interacts with the characteristics of the message, using clues from it to fit the new data into a place in the existing knowledge structure. The process is heavily influenced by the individual's existing knowledge and his analysis of the context (Anderson 1978:72). Richards calls this dynamic interaction between new and old knowledge *instantiation* (Anderson, Pichert, Goetz et al. 1976). In the process, a selection among possible variables goes on by both "bottom up" and "top down" methods. The perspective adopted by the subject has been found to influence both encoding and retrieval, as has the subject's prior experience, and the novelty of the material. All possible inferences are not instantiated, however. Whether or not a subject bothers to make a connection depends upon the significance of the material to the interpretation being constructed (Schallert 1982:27–34).

Because of its affirmation that people's knowledge, interests, and personal experiences serve as a higher order framework for the linkages between schemata and the interpretation of meaning, schema theory holds significant implications for educators. Among them:

- Ability to learn is based not so much upon stages of development as upon the existence of a framework of general schemata (prior knowledge) to which new knowledge can be linked. "Comprehension and therefore learning and memory, depend upon bringing to bear appropriate schemata" (Anderson 1977:421).

- Effective teachers will analyze students' existing knowledge and will access it to facilitate acquisition of new knowledge.

- Comprehension can be expanded progressively by helping students develop many connections between schemata, rather than being content to remain with only one or two linkages.

- Abstract schemata program individuals to generate concrete scenarios. In other words, comprehension of abstract messages depends on the individual's ability to instantiate (represent) abstractions with concrete representations consistent with the message. This statement is an important departure from previous thinking, i.e., that if the language of the text is abstract, the mental processes which go on with respect to it are abstract as well (Anderson 1977:423–24).

- The broader the range of situations a schema can potentially cover, the more loosely it will fit any one situation in all of its rich peculiarity. Well-developed schemata have great assimilative power (Anderson 1977:421, 429). For teachers, this highlights the importance of establishing generic concepts with care.

- Use of schema must involve *constructing interpretations* because every situation contains at least some novel characteristics. Herein lies the secret of successful transfer.

- Schemata change by gradual extension, articulation and refinement. However, didactic instruction will often fail to have a profound influence on deep-level schemata. The more fully developed the schema, the less likely it will be to change. Research indicates that the implications of new information will be resisted if its acceptance would require a major cognitive reorganization (Anderson 1977:424–25). This point has special application for cross-cultural educators.

- Apparent inconsistencies and counterexamples are often easily assimilated into the schemata to which a person is committed (Anderson 1977:425).

- The likelihood of schema change is maximized when a person recognizes a difficulty in his current position and comes to see that the difficulty can be handled within a different schema (Anderson 1977:427).

Teachers in cross-cultural classrooms can draw upon schema theory to identify core concepts, help students make connections between relevant ideas, and teach them to construct interpretations. It will also enable teachers to understand and sympathize more with students who have difficulty assimilating schema which contradict their previous suppositions.

2.3 Information processing

Robert Gagne, an educational psychologist thought of as a cognitivist and associationist of the verbal learning tradition, is known for his model of information processing. Skinner had proposed a simple stimulus-response sequence in learning. Gagne, in contrast, conceived a series of internal processes necessary for the sensing, selection, storage and retrieval of information. He listed the sequence as follows:

1. The sensory receptors (eyes, ears, skin) receive stimuli.
2. These are converted to neural impulses and delivered to . . .
3. A sensory register, which screens out irrelevant stimuli, such as background noise, and selects features which should be stored in the memory.
4. The selected impulses are sent to the short term memory, where they are either:
   a. Remembered for a few seconds and discarded (as in the case of a telephone number which is dialed and then forgotten), or
   b. Encoded semantically and sent to . . .
5. Storage in long term memory.

When the item is needed again,

6. A search is conducted in long term memory.
7. The item is retrieved and sent to short term memory.
8. From there it is sent to a response generator, which organizes the mind and muscles to respond. Lastly,
9. Effectors produce the required response, and the processing organism . . .
10. Awaits feedback, which will provide reinforcement and alert it to any further responses which may be necessary.

(Gagne 1985:76)

Gagne theorized that all knowledge is hierarchically ranked in a bottom-up order (although in later writings he was less sure as regards hierarchical ranking and gave more emphasis to prerequisite background knowledge as basic to learning). According to the hierarchical scheme, however, intellectual skills have the following levels; prequisite to each level are the levels below it.

Higher order rules

↑

Rules

↑

Concepts

↑

Discriminations

↑

Basic forms of learning: Associations and chains

(Gagne 1985:55)

Associations, the basic building blocks of this model, are simply two ideas which commonly associate with each other (Gagne 1985:23): roses and fragrance, for example, or doctor and hospital. A particular stimulus triggers a particular answer. *Chains* are sets of associations which occur in logical sequence—e.g., tying one's shoes, writing, or using a computer (Gagne 1985:36–38). *Discriminations* are the differences discerned between variations in objects and properties. *Concepts* are abstract ideas and definitions (e.g., justice; or a gallon of liquid consists of four quarts.) *Rules* state principles true of many cases, frequently cause and effect or correlations (e.g., warm air rises; when two vowels go walking, the first one does the talking.) *Higher order rules* combine simple rules into more complex processes; this is the domain in which problem solving takes place.

In contrast to Piaget, Gagne believes that every child can understand any rule (principle or generalization) if each of the prerequisite understandings—associations, discriminations, and concepts—is taught previously. Once a learner understands a concept, he or she is able to think with it without limitation. This idea was revolutionary at the time it was first proposed.

Gagne divides all human performance into five major categories, or learning outcomes:

1. Intellectual skills—procedural knowledge—which includes knowledge of language and other uses of symbols.
2. Verbal information—declarative knowledge—ability to state ideas and propositions.
3. Cognitive strategies—skills with which an individual manages his or her own learning, remembering and thinking. Cognitive strategies include techniques of analysis and problem solving.
4. Motor skills—the organized ability to execute movements, such as driving an automobile, or playing tennis.
5. Attitudes—mental states which influence the choices of personal actions.

(1985:47–48)

Conditions within the learner, and conditions within the learning situation vary with each of these five categories and enormously affect results.

For Gagne, student motivation occurs through incentive motivation (the use of rewards), task motivation (the satisfaction of obtaining new knowledge), achievement motivation (the tendency of learners to want to succeed), and through informing learners of the objective (so that they are able to match their performance with teacher expectations). Transfer of knowledge from one situation to another occurs through stimulus generalization when stimuli are similar or through concept generalization. (Cognitive strategies, classifying rules and cues for retrieval all play a part in concept generalization.) Forgetting occurs through interference, inhibition, and extinction.

Important to Gagne is the fact that when new material is processed by a learner, as indicated above, new memory structures are acquired. These new structures are what enable learners to display retention and transfer in terms of new performance (Gagne and White 1978:187).

This summary covers only the more salient features of information processing theory, but let us turn to its application for the teacher. Gagne saw important relationships between good teaching techniques and the sequence in which the brain processes information. He diagrammed them as follows:

Learning process	Instructional event
Reception	Gaining attention
Expectancy	Informing learners of the objective
Retrieval to working memory	Stimulating recall of prior knowledge
Selective perception	Presenting the stimulus material
Semantic encoding	Providing learning guidance
Responding	Eliciting performance
Reinforcement	Providing feedback
Retrieval and reinforcement	Assessing performance
Retrieval and generalization	Enhancing retention and transfer
	(Gagne 1985:246)

Gaining attention, Gagne suggested, means using some device—perhaps only a simple statement—which alerts the student to expect the lesson.

Expectancy directs attention to selected goals, enabling the learner to focus on the objective and providing a reason for him or her to be motivated.

Retrieval of prior knowledge to working memory is accomplished by reminders and by advance organizers.

Selective perception is achieved by presenting the lesson material very clearly and carefully so that the important items are in obvious focus.

Encoding is enhanced by the use of questions, and practice of different types, sufficient for the learner to gain control of the new material.

Response is elicited, first in practices, with test-like questions, then in individual work.

Reinforcement is provided through immediate feedback. More recent studies have indicated that retention is greater when teachers can devise a way for each student to answer each practice question (e.g., by raising hands or by pointing to an answer on an answer sheet) and to be informed immediately whether his answer is correct—or if not, what the correct answer should be.

Cueing retrieval can often be accomplished by providing students a mnemonic which they may use to remind themselves of the answer and by accustoming them to answer questions which require transfer and application of knowledge.

McKenzie, a student of Gagne, has developed a slightly modified version of Gagne's outline and instructional strategies for teaching the different types of knowledge (McKenzie 1974, 1979, 1980).

For teachers of cross-cultural classrooms, Gagne's instructional events provide an outline and checklist which can help to improve teaching effectiveness and, in consequence, to enhance learner achievement and satisfaction.

2.4 Social learning theory

Albert Bandura, an educational psychologist who began as a behaviorist, came to recognize that in many cases anticipation of results before the fact (rather than reward or punishment after the fact) is sufficient to motivate behavior. He is now known as a cognitivist and as the originator of social learning theory (Bandura 1963, 1965, 1977, 1986), which seeks to explain how it is that society can transmit mores, values, and skills so effectively, even though the learners frequently are not conscious of having been taught. His descriptions of the thought processes inherent in social learning are of a different genre than the descriptions of Ausubel, Anderson, and Gagne. Since instructional techniques are also in strong focus, some educators tend to think of social learning theory as an educational methodology rather than a theory of cognition.

Social learning theory is perceptive and broad; the main tenets are summarized by Lefrancoise as follows:

1. Much human learning is a function of observing the behavior of others or of symbolic models.
2. We learn to imitate by being reinforced for so doing, and continued reinforcement maintains imitative behavior.

3. Imitation, or observational learning, can therefore be explained in terms of operant conditioning principles.

(1988:171)

Since social learning theory asserts that in reality "most human behavior is learned observationally through modelling" (Bandura 1977:22), it recognizes the powerful influence that significant others, such as parents or sports heroes, bring to bear upon our lives. It investigates the tremendous multiplicative potential of media models, such as film stars and television personalities. It also emphasizes the wide diversity of behaviors which can be modelled effectively—for example, rule-governed behavior, social and moral standards, styles, conventions, and innovations—for different purposes. "Modelling influences can serve as instructors, inhibitors, disinhibitors, facilitators, stimulus enhancers, and emotion arousers" (Bandura 1977:50). The sequence followed during effective modelling is identified as the following:

Attentional processes. To reach the learner, the modelling stimuli must command attention. They must be carefully tailored to be distinctive, appealing, appropriately complex (neither too hard nor too easy), common enough to be relevant, and of functional value. The learner must be physically capable of receiving and imitating the stimuli, have the interest to do so, and be convinced that it is possible to succeed if he or she attempts to imitate the action modelled. (See Reiser and Gagne 1982.)

Retention processes. For learners to profit from modelled behavior, they must remember what they have seen. Symbolic coding—usually verbal—helps learners retain the lesson. Vivid imagery can have the same effect, as does mental rehearsal and actual motor rehearsal of the action sequence.

Motor reproduction processes involve actual enactment of the modelled behavior. Complex procedures, such as golf or swimming, require a long period of skill approximation and refinement through self-correction and feedback.

Motivational processes. Even though behavior has been learned, it is not always enacted. Observed consequences, rewarding or unrewarding, influence people's performance of modelled behavior. People's tastes vary as well, resulting in different degrees of acceptance of a modelled behavior; so it is important to find motivational incentives which are indeed perceived as rewarding by the recipients.

Behavior, in the view of the social learning theorist, is learned symbolically and is accepted before it is performed, but three kinds of reinforcement encourage learning and maintenance of new behaviors.

1. External reinforcement—the provision of rewards which have positive value for the learner. Not everyone responds to a given reward in the

same way (even well-intended praise may embarrass a learner in certain settings); thus the exhortation to provide incentives which are indeed rewarding.

2. Vicarious reinforcement—positive or negative consequences of an act which a learner observes and learns from without having to undergo them personally. Seeing behavior rewarded increases an individual's tendency to accept and engage in that behavior. Seeing it punished increases one's tendency to avoid the behavior. Thus observed outcomes provide reference standards and can alter behavior in much the same way as directly experienced consequences (Bandura 1977:117–18).

3. Self reinforcement—people hold firmly to ideological positions which enable them to evaluate their own behavior, set self-prescribed standards, and reward themselves with rewards within their power to control when goals are reached. Behavioral standards for determining self-reinforcing rewards can be taught either directly or indirectly through modelling (Bandura 1977:128–38). Self-reinforcement is a necessary and wholesome function; however, since self-esteem is closely tied to attainment values (Bandura 1977:143), self-reinforcement can be dysfunctional if demands are set too high or self punishment is excessive. Another unwholesome manifestation of dysfunctional self-reinforcement occurs if reprehensible behavior is disengaged from self-evaluative consequences by the mechanisms of moral justification, palliative comparison, euphemistic labeling, minimizing consequences, and misplacing blame (Bandura 1977:156).

Social learning theory's value for teachers lies in its focus upon teaching and learning strategies which have proved successful in the society at large. Modelling may be the best way to teach certain behaviors and to warn against others. Teachers do well to take more advantage of it. For modelling to be successful, however, careful attention needs to be directed toward: (a) gaining attention, (b) making the learning memorable, (c) providing opportunities to practice, and (d) offering appropriate incentives.

Efficacy expectations will need to be established. Bandura suggests that pupils be helped to know that they are capable of tasks by (a) performance accomplishments (helping them do it), (b) vicarious experiences (observing someone else do it), (c) verbal persuasion (telling them they can do it), and (d) emotional arousal (Bandura 1977:80).

Reinforcement—internal, external, and vicarious—maintains behaviors. Forgetting occurs when a behavior is no longer reinforced. Pupils can be taught to set their own goals and reward themselves through appropriate self-reinforcement.

Teachers in ethnolinguistic minority classrooms can use personal modelling as a powerful teaching tool but can also draw upon puppets, student role play and dramatization, and modelling by official visitors, selected parents, community leaders, and public figures.

2.5 Conclusion

Continuing research by educational psychologists has yielded new knowledge about the way the brain processes information and how learning takes place. Ausubel proposed the theory of reception learning, emphasizing the importance of advance organizers which enable a student to categorize new information correctly and relate it to other concepts in meaningful ways. Richards, the developer of schema theory, provided understanding of the elaborate relationships which link concepts and proposed that comprehension can only develop as a learner relates a new concept to other concepts appropriately. Gagne presents a theory of information processing which helps teachers by defining different kinds of knowledge which can be taught with different types of lessons. Bandura's social learning theory emphasizes the importance of modelling in teaching and specifies how it can be implemented most effectively.

The principles presented in each theory have useful applications in Western classrooms, and it is presumed that they will also be useful cross-culturally. Further studies are much needed to devise and test culturally appropriate applications for information-processing principles. Improved comprehension and academic success among students of ethnolinguistic minorities should be a predictable result.

References

Anderson, Richard C. 1977. The notion of schemata and the educational enterprise. In R. C. Anderson, R. J. Spiro, and W. E. Montague (eds.), Schooling and the acquisition of knowledge, 415–31. Hillsdale, New Jersey: Lawrence Erlbaum.

———. 1978. Schema-directed processes in language comprehension. In Alan M. Lesgold, James W. Pellegrino, Spike D. Fokkema and Robert Glaser (eds.), Cognitive psychology and instruction, 67–82. New York: Plenum Press.

————, J. W. Pichert, E. T. Goetz, D. L. Schallert, K. V. Stevens, and S. R. Trollip. 1976. Instantiation of general terms. Journal of Verbal Learning and Verbal Behavior 15:667–79.

Ausubel, David P. 1963. The psychology of meaningful verbal learning. New York: Grune and Stratton.

————. 1967. Learning theory and classroom practice. Bulletin 1. Toronto: The Ontario Institute for Studies in Education.

————, Joseph D. Novak, and Helen Hanesian. 1978. Educational psychology: a cognitive view. New York: Holt, Rinehart and Winston.

Bandura, Albert. 1963. Social learning and personality development. New York: Holt, Rinehart and Winston.

————. 1965. Behavioral modifications through learning procedures. In Leonard Krasner and Leonard P. Ullman (eds.), Research in behavior modification, 310–40. New York: Holt, Rinehart and Winston.

————. 1977. Social learning theory. Englewood Cliffs, New Jersey: Prentice-Hall.

————. 1986. Social foundations of thought and action: a social cognitive theory. Englewood Cliffs, New Jersey: Prentice-Hall.

Gagne, Robert M. 1985. The conditions of learning and theory of instruction. New York: Rinehart and Winston.

———— and Richard T. White. 1978. Memory structures and learning outcomes. Review of Educational Research 48(2):187–222.

Lefrancois, Guy R. 1988. Psychology for teaching. Belmont, California: Wadsworth Publishing Company.

McKenzie, Gary R. 1974. A theory-based approach to inductive value clarification. Journal of Moral Education 4(1):47–62.

————. 1979. Data charts: a crutch for helping pupils organize reports. Language Arts 10:784–88.

————. 1980. Improving instruction through instructional design. Educational Leadership 5:664–68.

Reiser, Robert A., and Robert M. Gagne. 1982. Characteristics of media selection models. Review of Educational Research 52(4):499–512.

Schallert, Diane. 1982. The significance of knowledge. In W. Otto (ed.), Reading expository material, 13–45. New York: Academic Press.

3

Learning Styles and Teaching Methods

Investigation of the cognitive styles involved in learning began with the early philosophers, but a major resurgence of interest in the topic was sparked by the research of Herman A. Witkin and his colleagues. Their testing began in the late 1940s and resulted in the identification of field dependence and field independence as two major learning styles. (Witkin 1978:2)

Activity continued to increase during the 1950s, and over the years since then many learning styles have been identified. For example: Guilford (1950) introduced the concepts of convergent and divergent thinking. Luria (1966) researched sequential and simultaneous processing. Pask and Scott (1972) and Pask (1976a; 1976b) developed knowledge concerning holistic learners, serial learners, and "versatile learners," (i.e., bicognitive learners who demonstrate both holistic and serial skills). Dunn and Dunn (1978) explored environmental conditions, techniques which significantly affect learners of differing styles, and with Price developed five learning style inventory questionnaires which identify twenty-three different aspects of learning preferences (Dunn 1988:306–7).

Although the researchers have departed from different theoretical bases and have used different terms, a large core of commonalities has emerged, while at the same time each study has added additional information. This chapter attempts to draw the material together, beginning with the core patterns as presented in the model used by Witkin and his colleagues. Information from other models will be included at appropriate points. In a field so large and complex, no one theory of human learning can be absolutely definitive, but the combined picture brings us nearer to truth.

Various nomenclatures have been used for the two main styles of learning: field dependence and field independence (Witkin and colleagues); analytic and relational (Cohen 1969); field sensitive and field independent (Ramirez and Castaneda 1974); global and linear (Kindell and Hollman, forthcoming); generalizers and particularizers (Ausubel 1967). While the terms may contain subtle nuances, they retain much of the common core of meaning. In this paper they will be used synonymously in accord with the preferred use of the author quoted, or—reflecting the usage of a number of today's authors—the terms analytic and holistic may be employed.

Since the field is so broad, this chapter purposes to identify the major themes found in the literature concerning cognitive learning styles in relation to ethnic minorities and to teaching. A cognitive learning style (an individual's characteristic approach to and preferred way of learning) is differentiated from cognitive development (what the brain is able to do in successive stages of maturity), and from learning strategies (specific techniques used to promote learning, such as demonstration and group repetition). These distinctions are important because considerable confusion of terms is found in the literature.

3.1 Field dependence versus field independence

Reliable testing

After years of effort, Witkin and his colleagues succeeded in developing reliable tests for identifying cognitive learning style differences (Witkin 1974:103; 1976: 39–42, Witkin at al. 1977:2–6). Three of the most important were the following:

1. The *Rod-and-Frame* test. Subjects were asked to position a luminous rod in upright position while a luminous frame, which was the only point of reference in a totally darkened room, remained tilted.

2. The *Body-Adjustment* test. The subject, seated in a tilted room, was required to adjust his own body to upright position.

3. The *Embedded Figures* test. Geometric figures, which the subject had seen previously, were embedded in a more complex figure, and he was requested to locate them.

When these tasks were accomplished satisfactorily by a subject, he was said to be *field independent* (FI), since he had been able to perceive items as discrete from the organized field of which they were a part. Subjects who were not able to perform the tasks were said to be *field dependent* (FD), since the environment as a whole dominated their perception of its parts. The tests, however, showed great variation, so that Witkin and other researchers conceived of field dependence and field independence (FD/I) as two poles of a continuum along which each individual finds a place. Parts of already developed intelligence tests—for example, the block design portion of the Wechsler test, and the Figure Drawing Test, in which drawings of the human body are evaluated by the number of features differentiated—also proved useful in measuring field dependence.

At this point, it is important to notice that Witkin's tests were heavily based on physical senses (body adjustment) and visual discrimination (embedded figures) rather than the mental processes which occur during learning. Critics, not unreasonably, consider this a serious limitation of the FD/I theory, even though real-life experience offers much support for it.

Definition of cognitive styles

As a result of Witkin's findings, cognitive styles were defined as:

> ... the characteristic self-consistent modes of functioning found pervasively throughout an individual's cognitive, that is perceptual and intellectual, activities. They are ... manifestations ... of still broader dimensions of personal functioning, evident in similar form in many areas of the individual's psychological activity (Witkin 1974:99).

Messick put it more simply: "Cognitive styles are consistent individual differences in ways of organizing and processing information" (1978:5). Ausubel et al. confirm this definition (1978:203).

Characteristics

In an important article summarizing the knowledge accumulated to the date of writing, Cohen described FD/I cognitive styles with the terms *analytic* and *relational*. Extensive charts detailed sociobehavioral characteristics of each style. For example:

Analytic	Relational
Sensitivity to parts of objects	Sensitivity to global characteristics
Attitude more reflective	Response appears more impulsive
Deep concentration	Shallow concentration
Preference for social distance	Preference for social integration
Makes many abstractions	Makes few abstractions
Sees teacher as a source of information	Sees teacher as a person

(1969:844–52)

In Cohen's scheme cognitive styles are considered to be highly individual traits, independent of native ability, race, sex, and socioeconomic status (1969:829). Cognitive styles, however, directly affect learning (Cohen 1968:201).

Witkin (1978:25–29) agreed with Cohen's descriptions. He considered both FD and FI as process variables, pervasive dimensions of individual functioning, bipolar, and value neutral. His evidence also indicated that a person's cognitive style tends to remain stable over time and across domains (Witkin et al. 1977:7, 15).

Psychological differentiation

Witkin introduced the term psychological differentiation to describe the all-pervasive manifestations of a cognitive style. "Differentiation refers to the complexity of a structure of a psychological system ... Greater differentiation manifests itself ... in segregation of psychological activities within the organism ..." (1978:15).

Differentiation shows itself in a person's processes of hierarchical structuring, development of controls over impulse expression, self-nonself segregation, and the degrees of emphasis placed upon internal or external referents in processing information. When tests showed that women tend to be slightly more FD than men, Witkin et al. attributed this difference to psychological differentiation (1977:7). Many of these behavioral correlates were noted: e.g,. FD people tend to be more perceptive, expressive, warm, and people-oriented than peers with FI orientation, who are often more cool, analytical, and detached (Witkin et al. 1977:10–14). The differences frequently affect the types of occupations chosen (Witkin 1976:52–54). For example, FI people tend to choose careers in engineering, mechanics and technology, mathematics, and science. FD people tend to choose careers such as teaching, selling, personnel management, psychology, and counselling (Witkin 1976:47–57).

Human personality, however, is too complex to be entirely molded by one variable. We do well to be cautious as to the amount of weight we assign to the FD/I factor when contemplating personality and behavior.

Societal variance

Witkin's theories were applied in cross-cultural research prior to 1966 (Witkin 1967). Although FD/I is recognized to be an individual matter, it has also been realized that members of certain cultures tend to be predominantly one or the other (Chapelle and Roberts 1986:29).

Agrarian or authoritarian societies, which are usually highly so-
cialized and have strict rearing norms, tend to produce more field
dependent persons. Democratic, industrialized societies with more
relaxed rearing practices tend to produce more field independence (Hansen 1984:313, quoting Witkin and Goodenough
1981 and Berry 1976).

Field independence, then, tends to characterize many United States
citizens (Ramirez and Castaneda 1974:156), the Mende of Sierra Leone
(Witkin 1974:106–8) and the Eskimo (Witkin 1974:109–10). Mexican-
American children tend to be more field dependent (Ramirez and Castaneda 1974:79, 132–33), as do Black Americans (Cox and Ramirez 1981),
and members of certain native North American groups (Pepper and Henry
1984:4), Australian Aborigines (Harris 1982), minority groups of the
Peruvian jungle (Davis, 1987:2), and at least one ethnic culture of the Philippines (Bulmer 1983) and of Ghana (Lingenfelter and Gray 1981).

Cohen described differences in the organization of groups composed of
the different cognitive styles. Among them she lists:

Group Characteristics

Analytic: Formally organized	Relational: Shared functions
Critical functions formally attached to statuses	Critical functions widely defined and shared
Individual retains the right to refuse to act	Individual cannot refuse to act
Casual identification with the group	Intense identification with the group

(Cohen 1969:852–54)

Ramirez and Castaneda list the following variables which influence field-
sensitive style for Mexican-American children:

1. Socialization practices of parents (emphasis on respect for family, religious, and political authority).
2. Community characteristics (a field-sensitive type society).
3. Dominant language (Spanish).
4. Embeddedness in the family (strong maternal ties).

(1974:132–33)

More recently, Hansen studied the relationship between field dependence
and cloze test performance for 286 teenage subjects representing six Pacific

island cultures. The Group Embedded Figures Test revealed "striking differences between the groups sampled, not only in the level of field independence, but in the correlation between FD/I and sex as well" (1984:317). The Hawaiian students tested were found to be significantly more field independent than those tested from Samoa, Tonga, Tahiti, and Fiji (both native Fijians and Indian-Fijian students). The males were significantly more field independent than the females in all but the Hawaiian sampling.

Molding influences

The question of why cultures tend to be predominately composed of members who demonstrate the same FD or FI tendencies spurred another series of studies.

Seder (1957, reported in Witkin 1974:106) documented cognitive differences between Jewish boys in New York City, depending on the degree of differentiation demonstrated by their mothers. Seder's work was supported by Dawson (1963 and 1967), who compared Temne and Mende, two ethnolinguistic groups of Sierra Leone, and found that field dependence is fostered by heavy parental domination. Berry (1966a, 1966b) agreed, showing that Eskimos are very similar to Scots in field independence, due, it was presumed, to parental expectations of independence and also environmental conditions which require boys to develop keen visual discrimination.

Evaluating these studies, Witkin concluded that social conditioning contributes to FD or FI, but that socioeconomic status does not (1969:691–701; 1974:106–10, 116–17). Support for this statement is provided by Lingenfelter and Gray who speak of societies in which one cognitive style is rewarded more than the other. As a result, the preferred style flourishes within the society, while the less esteemed style is repressed. To illustrate, they cite this striking experience:

> Take ... the case of the two Micronesian boys who lived for six years in the home of one of the authors. Although related, one was inclined to be relational while the other favored the analytic. Student A did very well in the American school system because he possessed a strong ability to analyze and abstract. Student R, although intelligent, had a great deal more difficulty understanding the demands of college work. However, when the two students returned to Micronesia, Student R adapted fairly quickly and is a real credit to his father. His ability to grasp a situation in its context has helped him immensely in his job. Student A, on the other hand, has had great difficulties in adjusting to the cultural demands. In Micronesia his ability to abstract and question labels

him a 'smart aleck,' and older people do not take too kindly to his ideas for change (1981:15–16).

Cox and Ramirez (1981:62–63) identify three factors—the task, the situation, and the materials—which influence the ways children learn to behave. Parents' teaching styles, they posit, are of basic importance in setting the direction of a child's learning preference. Parental teaching styles are heavily influenced by cultural values. Thus, the flow of influence is shown in the diagram below.

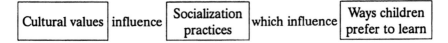

Laosa, while agreeing that childhood socialization practices characteristic of certain cultures tend to foster the development of particular cognitive styles, warns that it is risky to generalize group findings to individuals. He then raises a further question:

> If ... characteristic cognitive styles are adaptive to the ecological and cultural settings which groups occupy in a society, what happens to these differences during the process of culture contact and social change? There is some evidence that cognitive styles change as a result of acculturation ... (1977:28).

Capacity for development

Witkin (1974:100–101) described mental processes as passing through developmental stages from the simple global perception of a field to an articulated perception in which discrete items are perceived, yet structure is imposed upon the whole. Greenfield's studies among the Wolof of Senegal support the statement (Greenfield and Bruner 1966:104–5, citing studies done in 1963–1964). Greenfield tested rural unschooled Wolof children, bush school children, and city children for grouping concepts, and reported:

> ... It is always the schooling variable that makes qualitative differences in directions of growth. Wolof children who have been to school are more different intellectually from unschooled children living in the same bush village than they are from city children in the same country or from ... Brookline (Massachusetts) (1966:104).

Greenfield and Bruner (1966:104) mention other studies demonstrating the huge impact of school which were carried out in the Belgian Congo

(Cryns 1962) and South Africa (Biesheuvel 1949). Experience in the Peruvian Amazon also indicates that strategies for field articulation can be learned, if they are made explicit and presented slowly (Davis 1981: 231–32). An experience from Ghana illustrates this.

Among the Bulsa people, English served as both the official and the prestige language, and children attended English speaking schools. The dropout rate was high and the retention rate correspondingly low. Seeking to capitalize on the Bulsa ability to memorize wholes, Claire Gray wrote a new primer in which only sixteen words were presented. In a second book the simple frame "This is" was added. A few key words were broken down into syllables, but only those in which the component parts had meanings in themselves. Aided by the meaning, students quickly assimilated these breakdowns. Book three contained simple stories and expanded the vocabulary to about 80 words, but only a few more words were broken down. In book four, students were shown how the technique of breaking down words into meaningful parts could be transferred to words in which syllables did not have meaning. By then, the concept of analysis and synthesis had been established, and students progressed without further difficulty (Lingenfelter and Gray 1981:16–17).

In this regard, Pepper and Henry comment that although it is desirable to capitalize on students' learning styles when presenting new concepts at least sixty-five percent of the time, it is also necessary, twenty-five to thirty-five percent of the time, to help them acquire different learning styles so the student may continue to grow intellectually. "Too often, Indian students make normal or above-normal academic gains while attending a 'sheltered' school only to fail once they leave that situation...Is it not our responsibility to stretch the Indian student's learning styles...to keep from locking our Indian students into a certain mold" (Pepper and Henry c. 1984:18–19).

3.2 Learning styles and educability

I.Q. Tests

Because Cohen found that relational learners tended to score lower on I.Q. tests, she made a study of nonverbal measures of intelligence. Contrary to the belief that only verbal testing contains a culture-bound component while nonverbal instruments concentrate on logical reasoning, she found that "it is in the very nature of these logical sequences that the most culture-bound aspects of the middle class or 'analytic' way of thinking are carried" (1969:840).

Supporting her position were test results from sixty-six ninth and tenth grade pupils of average or better intelligence. The more intelligent, highly relational pupils scored very low on two achievement subtests of the Project Talent Achievement Inventory (15th to 20th percentiles) but did extremely well on two sets of concrete problems (90th to 95th percentiles). Cohen concluded that to learn and perform well, highly relational students need concrete material and that I.Q. tests are discriminatory against them in proportion to the level of abstraction demanded.

Since cognitive styles are not adequately measured by I.Q. tests, Witkin suggests that I.Q. testing might be replaced with cognitive style testing (1976:70–71).

Scholastic discrimination

Cohen's research identified a further source of problem for relational learners: Because Western school systems are built on the analytic (FI) model, the relational (FD) learner is "unlikely to be rewarded in the school setting regardless of his native abilities and even if his information repertoire and background of experience are adequate" (Cohen 1969:830). Using a battery of psychological, linguistic and attitudinal tests, Cohen isolated four clear response types:

1. High-relational pupils: poor school achievers, or underachievers
2. High-analytic pupils: good school achievers
3. Middle-range relational and analytic pupils: middle-range achievers
4. High-analytic and high-field-dependent pupils: middle-range achievers who demonstrated conflicting responses and confusion.
(1968:209)

Her evidence supported Witkin's conclusion that cognitive styles are influenced by early family and group experiences. However, Cohen's testing of 500 ninth graders did not provide any evidence that cognitive style is related to native ability (1969:838).

Pepper and Henry pinpoint the scholastic disadvantage native American FD learners suffer: "As a rule, Indian students learn faster when the teaching style uses the concrete approach and moves to the abstract—from practice to theory. Most schools follow the European American model from theory to practice" (c. 1984:16).

Speaking of traditional learning styles among the Australian Aborigines, Harris lists characteristics which appear to be highly relational:

Informal learning, conducted by various relatives largely through nonverbal means, without specifically arranged buildings, over a period of years, as an unconscious process growing out of the needs of subsistence living.

Observation and imitation (rather than verbal instruction).

Personal trial-and-error (rather than verbal instruction).

Orientation to persons (rather than to information).

Learning through wholes (rather than parts), or through successive approximations to efficient end products (rather than through sequencing of skills).

Acceptance of the universe as a "given" and not something open to change or manipulation.

Use of persistence and repetition instead of analysis as a problem-solving approach.

Avoidance of verbal confrontation.

Resistance to asking questions, especially self-obvious or rhetorical questions, and hypothetical questions

(1982:129–33).

These characteristics have consistently caused Aboriginal students to place poorly in comparison to European peers. That this fact has nothing to do with innate intelligence is indicated by a study carried out by Klich and Davidson in which seventy-six children from two communities in the remote northwest desert area of South Australia and ninety-one white Australian children from rural New South Wales were given a battery of eleven tests. Their conclusion: no apparent difference in the underlying pattern of cognitive processing functions between these samples of Aboriginal and non-Aboriginal children could be statistically established (1984:191).

Domains of learning affected

In a review of perceptions acquired up to 1977, Witkin et al. enumerate domains of learning affected by cognitive styles (1977:17–27).

Social material

Witkin et al. (1977:18–19, quoting studies undertaken by Ruble and Nakamura (1972), Crutchfield et al. (1958), and Fitzgibbons et al. (1965), cite evidence that field dependent individuals—both children and adults—were better at picking up and utilizing social cues, remembering faces, and learning social material peripheral to a task on which they were concentrating. Witkin's conclusion: "Field dependent persons are better at remembering social material and . . . this superiority is based on their selective attention to social material." They tend to be more effective in tasks or situations which involve relevant social cues (Ruble and Nakamura 1972).

Somewhat in the same vein, Bulmer (1983:24–30) cites an experience from the Kalinga of the Philippines in which it has been necessary to provide the appropriate social context in order for learning to go forward. Among the Kalinga, people are the goal, and relationships are extremely important. When differences arise, go-betweens are enlisted to avoid shaming anyone. To be able to study happily, students cannot be isolated but need to work in a homogeneous group with others with whom they normally interact in the village. Class times must be social times with freedom for discussion of students' interests; students must be permitted to copy from and help each other; no one must ever be embarrassed or shamed, and allowance must be made for interruptions such as ceremonies, visitors, and work projects.

Harris (1982:132) recounts a similar experience which emphasized for him that Australian Aboriginal learning involves orientation to persons (most often close relatives) rather than to information. For two months he and his wife had been assisting a head teacher in an Aboriginal Writers' Workshop which was being conducted for a group of young Aboriginal women. When the head teacher left for a week of vacation, progress virtually ceased although the students continued to attend class. Thinking that the language barrier might be the problem, even though the students were reasonably fluent in English, the Harrises arranged for the assistance of a teacher who spoke the Aboriginal language. The students and new teacher got on well, but it made very little difference to the writing program. The classes did not return to normal until the original teacher returned.

Harris also gives insight into the types of group experiences which are meaningful for tradition-oriented, field dependent students:

> Group sharing of learning experiences—especially of peer groups—is common in Aboriginal society, with oral group chanting, for example, being a common means of learning lengthy song cycles, and with most learning in ceremonial activities or food gathering activities taking place in groups. Members of groups are thus often used to carrying each other, as it were. One reason Aboriginal people do not, relatively speaking, mind repetitious activity is that they often do it in the company of groups of which they enjoy being a part . . . Another important aspect . . . is that of

supplying the student with the answer, as it were, nearly all the time, rather than requiring the students to struggle on their own towards mastery of each bit... Teachers of Aboriginal students will need to decide whether giving the answers is really 'cheating' or poor teaching method, or whether in fact it is very often merely another way of ultimately getting to the same goal (1980:19).

Reinforcement

Since students with "a global style tend to rely more on external referents for self-definition... field dependent students would be more likely to require externally defined goals and reinforcements than field independent students" (Witkin et al. 1977:19). FD individuals are also more affected by criticism since their security derives from being in harmony with others. Witkin and his colleagues cite a number of studies in which FI subjects performed somewhat better than field dependent children when reinforcement was abstract, but if rewards were either material or social, FD children did equally well. In contrast, FI persons tend to learn more under conditions of intrinsic motivation (1977:19-20).

Reporting substantiating evidence from the FD Kalinga of the Philippines, Bulmer writes:

Earned prestige is a great motivating force for literacy, and education is already seen as a means of earning it. Achievement must be acknowledged and it is very important to give certificates and other recognition at a graduation ceremony. The fact that the district government school supervisor came to our adult graduation in Mallango... gave the adults a tremendous boost (1983:29).

Organization

According to Witkin et al. (1977:21-22), FI students tend to impose structure on material which lacks clear inherent structure and to make use of cues which they themselves develop to aid learning. FD students have more difficulty learning unstructured material, as they do not as easily devise ways of organizing or unifying the concepts; neither do they usually test hypotheses as a FI student might do. The authors refer to a 1968 study by Fleming et al. in which subjects were asked to learn words in both superordinate sequences (i.e., animal, vertebrate, man) and subordinate (man, vertebrate, animal). In superordinate sequences, the first word acted as an organizational title; it was hypothesized that the subordinate series, which lacked this cue, would prove more difficult for FD subjects. As predicted, FD students were able to recall fewer of the subordinate series examples, although they equalled FI subjects in recall of the superordinate series.

Reporting on a study by a colleague, Walter Emmerich, Witkin et al. state that teachers found FD students did better when they were provided with a plan. "Greater need of field-dependent persons for externally provided structure is a general characteristic of their behavior" (1977:23).

Another evidence of the greater need of FD persons for externally provided structure was reported by Greene (1972) and cited by Witkin and colleagues:

> Therapists significantly more often choose supportive therapy for their FD patients and modifying therapy for their FI patients . . . In supportive therapy the therapist assumes greater responsibility for providing structure for the therapeutic process, whereas in modifying therapy, the patient himself plays a part in determining the content and progress of the process (1977:23).

Not only individuals, but some societies as a whole, evidence highly developed organizing skills. MacArthur found that Canadian Eskimos and northern Indians, both of whom are representatives of hunting and gathering societies, "were more FI, that is, more able to impose a structure on a field when it has little inherent organization (e.g., unmapped territory), as a result of their living style and child rearing practices" (1968, quoted in More 1984:6).

Weitz " . . . studied two Indian cultural groups, Algonkian and Athapaskan, and within these groups separated out urban, transitional, and traditional groups as well as male-female and older-younger. She found that the overall group scored very high on FI" (1971, quoted in More 1984:6).

Seemingly contradictory is the well-documented report that the field dependent Australian Aborigines have exceptional skills in tracking and geographic orientation despite the vast, and, to Western eyes, apparently featureless terrain of central Australia:

> What became evident to Lewis was that under normal conditions Aborigines utilized a complex 'topographical schema' (Gibson 1950) relying primarily on (a) knowledge of important landmarks; (b) familiarity with the body of mythical stories associated with those landmarks; and (c) the use of dynamic mental maps . . . (Lewis 1976a in Klich and Davidson 1984:172).

Thus, Lewis concluded that:

> The highly developed visual-spatial orientation skills of the desert Aborigines could be attributed to the use of complex mapping

processes following 'terrestial conditioning' through emotional and spiritual links with the land patterned by networks of mythical events (Lewis 1976b in Klich and Davidson 1984:173).

The ability of the otherwise FD-type Aborigines to impose structure on the desert seems to be the product of a learned process, required by the need for survival and supported by broad structuring (landmarks) reinforced by religious beliefs.

Concept attainment

Educators accept two models of concept attainment: hypothesis testing (learning by trying) and the spectator approach (learning by observation). Witkin et al. report a study by Nebelkopf and Dreyer (1973) which supports the hypothesis that FI persons tend to use the hypothesis testing model most frequently, and FD persons the spectator approach. The evidence also suggests that when FD persons do use a hypothesis testing approach, they "form hypotheses on a different basis than do FI persons" (Witkin et al. 1977:24–25).

Supporting evidence for the use of the spectator approach among certain ethnic minorities comes from Peru:

> In some of the [jungle] cultures with which we are familiar, one learns by watching. Children observe their parents, and others, for as long as necessary until they feel sure that they have mastered the techniques of the process in question. Explanations are not expected and are seldom given, yet when the child makes his first attempt, he ordinarily does very well. It is a great embarrassment to perform poorly; it demonstrates pride and too much haste (Davis 1981:231).

Harris reports that one of the major learning processes of the Australian Aboriginal is observation and imitation rather than verbal instruction, either oral or written. For example:

> M (aged forty five) and his three sons, aged eleven, nine and six years, were cutting stringy-bark trees, four to five inches in diameter, for didgeridoos which M wanted to make to sell in the craft shop. M went up to each potential tree and gazed carefully up its length, looking for any dead branches or holes that might indicate a hollow tree. Each of the sons followed his gaze, especially the elder two boys, often going to the same side of the tree at which M was standing so that they could have the same viewing position. When M moved round the tree, still looking up at the trunk, the boys sometimes moved with him. M muttered to himself

from time to time, but did not say anything to the boys. Every time a tree fell, the boys went over eagerly to see if it was hollow. Once when M was sitting having a rest, each of the two elder boys tried to cut a tree down but the axe was too heavy for them and they soon gave up.

Virtually all survival skills, social skills and much learning of artistic skills ... are learned through observation and imitation ... (Aboriginal people are highly verbal but talk has more of a social than a teaching function.) (1982:130–31).

Swisher and Deyhle (1987:345–54) cite examples of native North American groups who prefer to learn by observation and mental rehearsal and by avoiding competition. In the school, student-initiated conversation and contacts with the teacher are the norm. The students also respond better to painstaking, patient, personalized explanations, which capitalize on their highly-developed visual skills.

Cue salience

Witkin et al. (1977:25–27) cite studies by Bruner et al., Goodenough and others which point out that FD learners tend to use fewer of the cues available in a field than do FI students. They may also have difficulty dissociating cues which have had a history of relevance in their experience from new situations in which they are not relevant. Witkin suggests that their learning may be improved by instructions which guide them to look for the appropriate clues and by encouragement to search for alternate ways of dealing with problems. The recent literature seems to have no clear examples illustrating this observation.

3.3 Additional research

Other learning styles

While FD/FI has been the focus of much of the research related to cognitive styles, scholars agree that there are other styles. Valencia names twelve which appear in the literature:

1. Analyzing: facility in concentrating on details and seeing separate parts of an object or situation (Tyler 1965).

2. Synthesizing: facility in seeing the field as an integrated whole; not so much facility in perceiving details (Tyler 1965).

3. Convergent thinking: facility in reaching logical conclusions based on conventional reasoning; scientific reasoning; working problems that have clear cut answers (Kogan 1979).

4. Divergent thinking: facility in generating alternative possibilities and solutions to problems, also in imaginative thinking.

5. Cognitive complexity: facility in organizing information in hierarchical fashion; tendency to perform well on tasks which require vertical analysis of relations between dimensions (Kogan 1979).

6. Cognitive simplicity: tendency to use dimensions of difference when integrating information (Kogan 1979).

7. Field dependence: facility in seeing complex perceptual fields as a whole. Tendency to give greater attention to persons and things, to be more socially perceptive and responsive to external directions. Preference for lessons prefaced with supportive assurances from the teacher, problem solving strategies modeled by the teacher, and a humanized instructional model.

8. Field independence: tendency to differentiate stimuli found within a perceptual field. Preference for tasks requiring factional information and problems based on analytical processes. Preference for individual and independent learning, with the teacher serving as a resource person rather than a model.

9. Leveling: facility in assimilating new stimuli into already established cognitive organization but not always in perceiving the differences between the old and the new (Tyler 1965).

10. Sharpening: facility in differentiating new and old, in noticing changes, in creating new categories (Tyler 1965).

11. Scanning: facility in proceeding through a maze of detail with uniform awareness, mentally organizing from broad to narrow.

12. Focusing: facility in locating and focusing upon a few key details; thus performance is often prompt and correct. Important peripheral cues may be missed, however (Rice 1979).

(1980–81:62–63)

Witkin lists as well: Constricted versus flexible control, strong versus weak automatization, conceptualizing, and reflection versus impulsivity (1978:4). Ausburn and Ausburn add visual versus haptic (1978:351).

Brown considers reflectivity and impulsivity (closely related to systematicity and intuition), tolerance and intolerance of ambiguity, broad and narrow categorization width, and skeletonization and embroidery to be other little-researched but bonafide cognitive styles (1980:89–98).

More finds a simultaneous versus successive category useful when seeking to understand the performance of certain native American children, who on tests conducted by Krywaniuk (1974), Das, Manos and Kanungo (1975), and Kaufman (1983), scored higher on simultaneous measures and lower on successive measures than did white students. Preliminary results from testing carried out by More and colleagues in British Columbia indicate that "Indian students have a relative strength in simultaneous processing," which raises a question concerning phonic reading programs in which the emphasis is on successive processing (1984:7).

Cahir (1981:24) identifies a verbal versus visual cognitive dichotomy which he considers to be equally as important as FD/I. He has found children from certain cultural groups, among them some native Americans, to be more responsive to information presented visually than verbally.

Ausubel (1967) also lists most of the above categories, with some explanation of each, but feels "the most significant dimension of cognitive style that has implications for subject-matter learning . . . is the tendency for individuals to be generalizers or particularizers or to be somewhere between these extremes on a continuum" (Ausubel et al. 1978:204).

Inductive versus deductive learning preferences appear to be closely linked to global versus analytic learning styles. At least some educators consider the inductive-deductive dichotomy to reflect thought processes better than FD/I distinctions, to be more stable across students and teachers, and to subsume field dependence and field independence (Dr. Dolores Cardenas, personal conversation). This appears to differ from Piaget's linking of inductive learning with the stage of concrete operations, and hypothetico-deductive learning with the formal operations stage (Kolb 1984:25). Abstract thinking is part of both inductive and deductive teaching as it is used in the U.S. school system today.

Reinert, after testing over one thousand students in the Seattle area, has identified four ways in which people internalize new information. He classified these as learning styles and suggests that foreign language learners capitalize upon their preferred style to further their progress.

1. By forming a mental image of the object or activity.
2. By forming a mental image of the word spelled out.
3. By receiving meaning from the sound, without any visualization.
4. By sensing a fleeting kinesthetic reaction, either emotional or physical.

(1976:161)

Hemispheric dominance

Subsequent to Witkin's and Cohen's work, a physiological explanation for learning styles was advanced: that differences could be attributed to specialization of the right and left brain hemispheres. Neurological and psychoneurological testing with brain-damaged patients had indicated that cerebral specialization could be categorized, at least for certain functions.

Left Hemisphere	Right Hemisphere
Language	Spatial relations
Symbolism and abstraction	Concrete representation
Fine temporal order judgments; time consciousness	Grouping of parts into wholes; perceiving patterns and structures
Sequencing.	Simultaneous processing
Analysis: figuring things out step by step	Analogic: seeing likenesses between things

So many researchers and authors pursued the topic that a complete listing is impossible. The following will serve as examples: Sperry 1969; Ten Houten 1971; Doyle, Ornstein and Galin 1974; Krashen 1976; Edwards 1979; Fadley and Hosler 1979 and 1983; McKeever 1981; Springer and Deutsch 1981; Polich 1982.

Much of the material was helpful, but after a time questions were raised. Albert and Obler (1978), from their testing with bilinguals in Israel, have presented strong evidence that although the left hemisphere does appear to control language in monolingual subjects, bilingual and multilingual subjects show language control in the right hemisphere as well. Levy, a biopsychologist from the University of Chicago, argues that the two hemispheres of the brain do not function independently, and that there is no evidence of people's being purely "left brained" or "right brained." "Normal people have ... one gloriously differentiated brain, with each hemisphere contributing its specialized abilities"

(1985:44). Chrisjohn and Peters from the Department of Psychology, University of Guelph state that "the most thoughtful and respected thinkers in the area emphasize beyond everything else, the importance not of the separate contributions of the left and right hemispheres of the brain, but of the collaboration of the two hemispheres in the guidance of behavior" (1984, quoting Kinsbourne 1982).

It appears that the theory of hemispheric dominance needs to be held with some reservations, since it is now felt that brain functioning is too complex and plastic to be defined so categorically.

3.4 Holistic instruction

Slowly, instructional techniques appropriate for holistic learners are being researched. The National Association of Secondary Principals has compiled information to aid school administrators and teachers in diagnosing and prescribing programs. The Association has also listed some of the evaluative instruments (tests and inventories) available to help teachers identify students' learning styles (1979:133). As a further aid, Hernandez (1989:121–25) presents an informal learning style inventory which provides a rough profile of learning and teaching style. A helpful book, *Unicorns are real: a right-brained approach to learning* (Meister Vitale 1985), lists ideas for teaching colors, reading processes, writing, math operations, organization, grammar, music, and provides titles of other sources. Carbo, Dunn, and Dunn (1986) and McCarthy (1980) supply additional procedures.

An example

An anecdote by Harris illustrates how one holistic type learning program has been carried out:

> I would like now to illustrate . . . how one modern methodology has (quite by accident because it was developed in France for international businessmen) many Aboriginal learning processes in it and has been highly successful with at least one group of Aboriginal adults. In 1977, a demonstrator of the Structuro Global Audio Visual method of teaching oral English . . . worked at Milingimbi for six weeks. This program placed Aborigines in simulated settings where they could learn the types of dialogues necessary to get by in white society. Through the repeated use of films of dialogues, a tape recorder and an intonation machine, students were able by means of successive approximations of the

efficient end products (through mime and continuous attempts at role playing the dialogues) to gain confidence in speaking some practical English. The learning circumstances were highly social. Students spent most of their time trying to talk to other students (using phrases and sentences from the film they had just seen), learning by experience, and by constantly trying in a nontesting, nonembarrassing context. Failure was not possible because a student was able to mime out the dialogue when the words wouldn't come. Students also had some choice of exactly when and how they responded, although the individual was actually carried along in a group surge of activity.

I have worked with and seen Aboriginal adult education classes where after two or three sessions, attendance dwindled away to nothing. After six weeks at three hours per day most of the men and women involved in the All's Well course were still keen. I ascribe the response of the Aboriginal adults in this program to high initial motivation, very skilled teaching, and to the many Aboriginal features and learning processes in this learning activity: there was a group and clan loyalty, i.e., *person* orientation; the sessions were enjoyable, i.e., *ends* in themselves and not perceived merely as dull practice sessions for later ends; there was no clear spectator-actor distinction (which parallels Aboriginal dance situations); and there was much *observation, repetition, imitation; learning by doing, personal trial and error;* all in a nonthreatening context. There was no formal testing in the body of the program, and Aboriginal facility for and love of drama was used to the full. There was no direct questioning, no threat to Aboriginal felt rights to independent action, no embarrassment of individuals in front of groups and no lengthy verbal instruction. (1982:136).

Holistic instructional techniques

FI/FS teaching and learning strategies

Ramirez and Castaneda (1974:133–40) and Herold, Ramirez and Castaneda (1974:72–73) have observed and charted field-independent and field-sensitive teaching strategies and learning behaviors. Their books are a must for the cross-cultural teacher. Hernandez (1989:131–33) also lists learning strategies adapted from Weinstein and Mayer (1986). Kaulback (1984) contributes recommendations for Native Americans gleaned from the literature, as do Pepper and Henry (1984:59).

FI/FD Curriculum

Herold et al. (1974:74–75) have also summarized important differences between field-sensitive and field-independent curricula.

They comment that the traditional classroom arrangement with desks in rows is probably better suited to FI teaching, while small tables and activity centers are more conducive to field-sensitive learners. Kolb (1984) extends discussion to the application of learning style principles in an experiential model. Baumann (1984) suggests ways in which teachers can help students grasp main ideas.

Holistic lesson plans

Kindell and Hollman (forthcoming), building upon Baumann (1984), Herold, Ramirez and Castaneda (1974), and experience at Summer Institute of Linguistics training courses in both Brazil (Wieseman 1978) and England, have developed a lesson plan which applies global teaching strategies. It is particularly designed for the teaching of linguistics, but is applicable to analytical subjects such as math and science and is adaptable for other subjects as well. The components are:

- Introduction: A brief overview, designed to give students a clear understanding of the content and purpose of the lesson.

- Direct instruction: New knowledge is presented clearly beginning with the whole and moving to the parts. Demonstration and modelling are important ingredients. Questions are invited and clarifications given in a nonthreatening way. No intuitive leaps are expected.

- Teacher directed application: The students practice the new procedure with the teacher, who gives both guidance and feedback. The model presented should be used exactly; no leaps of knowledge should be required.

- Independent practice: Students practice as individuals or as a group, while the teacher serves as a resource. Again, the model should be followed exactly.

- Independent application: Students apply the new knowledge independently, and preferably as individuals. They should now be ready to cope with variations in the model and to apply new concepts or procedures.

Kindell and Hollman (personal conversation) prefer to use the terms *linear* and *global*, considering them to be less pejorative than the terms FI/FD. Their experience indicates that linear learners tend to demonstrate speed and facility in learning individual pieces of information and using them to build whole concepts. Global learners tend to be skilled in understanding the large picture and in relating wholes to each other. For them, as each new piece of information is learned it must be accommodated into a total scheme and related to every other piece of information already received. For this reason, global learners may require a little more time to acquire knowledge, and also need to practice a basic model until they are sure that they have understood the principles correctly. Thereafter, they can be expected to demonstrate considerable ability and creativity in the application of their knowledge. Of course, a range of intelligence and creativity is to be expected among both FI and FD learners, consistent with that of the general population.

Kindell and Hollman's lesson plan coincides closely with a model developed in the Peruvian jungle for bilingual schools among twenty-eight ethnolinguistic minority groups. Lessons for math, science, history, and geography follow the following format, beginning at grade three level:

1. Review of previously taught material.
2. Motivation. Something interesting to introduce the lesson.
3. Observation. Students observe while the teacher demonstrates, models, explains, and answers questions.
4. Elaboration. The teacher shows how the new knowledge can be represented—with numbers, diagrams, graphs, or the procedure for writing up solutions to problems.
5. Expression. Students practice the procedure until they are able to do it independently, in writing. Question format is not varied until they control the model.

(Davis and Jakway 1983:82–86).

Bowen and Bowen (1989) have applied global learning studies to the teaching of African seminary students and have produced a list of helpful methods. See also Schooling (1984 and 1987) for suggestions regarding the training of mother-tongue translators and Sodemann (1987) for a discussion of the use of lectures and memorization in the cross-cultural setting.

Teacher training

Westerners involved in training native teachers from largely holistic societies have often encountered difficulties. Graham offers valuable insights gleaned from the Australian experience. She especially recommends the building of rapport through the creation of team situations in which Westerners and non-Westerners meet as equals; working in groups of more than two; modeling by experienced members of the team, each in his or her own area of expertise; sensitivity to nonverbal communication and cultural cues; and use of the vernacular language (1980a:34–35).

Graham has developed a culturally relevant teachers' guide (1980b) and a check list of practical suggestions to promote effective cross-cultural communication (1980a), which is applicable in many countries besides Australia. (See Appendix B.)

At the university level, McEachern and Kirkness (1987) have developed a teacher education model appropriate for the British Columbia Native Indian Teacher Education Programme. The course requirements include the normal graduation requirements (with differences in the sequencing of courses), additional Indian studies, and twelve weeks of practicum in each of the first two years of the program to accommodate students who learn better by doing than by hearing.

Curriculum organization and evaluation

Banks (1988:273–92) lists broad curriculum guidelines for multiethnic education in large school systems. Included are recommendations that the multiethnic curriculum should help students develop values which support ethnic pluralism; should increase decision-making abilities, social-participation skills, and sense of political efficacy; and should help students interpret events from diverse ethnic perspectives.

Banks also recommends (1988:293–301) a multiethnic education inventory titled *Evaluation Guidelines for Multicultural-Multiracial Education* (Arlington, Virginia: National Study of School Evaluation, 1973:25–33). This evaluation includes checklists for the ethnic-racial balance of the staff, conduct of the teachers and administrators, school organization and grouping, the formal curriculum, learning materials, and special education.

3.5 Bicognitive development

Every individual has need to draw upon both holistic and analytic techniques to be successful in the tasks of life, for each style has its strengths and its limitations and the most effective functioning is achieved by calling upon each as appropriate.

> Competent and effective functioning in both cognitive styles im-
> plies integration . . . of the affective and cognitive domains. The
> goal that children become more versatile and adaptable to the
> increasingly complex demands of life . . . may be reached by help-
> ing them develop the ability . . . to draw upon both styles at any
> given time (Castaneda and Gray 1974:206).

Since teachers are faced with both types of students in their classrooms, Ramirez and Castaneda (1974:150–51) recommend that teachers cultivate both teaching styles in order to reach all the pupils, and to stimulate bicognitive functioning. They list unadaptive FI behavior as excessive concern with rivalry and excessive independence, whereas behaviors which promote success include the ability to compete individually, to work independently, to use a discovery approach and to deal with math and science abstractions. Unadaptive field-sensitive behaviors are distractability and overreliance on a teacher's approval. Behaviors which promote success for the field-sensitive student are the ability to work cooperatively, sensitivity to others' feelings and to a wide variety of cues, and ability to learn by modeling and imitation. Understanding of the opposite style is often lacking; both types of individuals need to learn to understand and respect, and also to cultivate, the strengths oi the other.

Herold, Ramirez and Castaneda suggest that to help a student develop bicognitive skills the teacher can:

1. Group students, matching instruction to their preferred style.
2. Gradually introduce performance in the unfamiliar style (through association with peers of that style).
3. Work with the child to observe how he or she is responding and developing in the new behavior. This presupposes the student's understanding of and cooperation in the process.

(1974:58)

In addition to the above, Williams (1983) discusses modes of thinking and how to teach students process awareness. Davis and Pyatskowit (1976) treat bicognitive education from the point of view of the Menominee Community School (Menominee reservation, northern Wisconsin). They list eight Menominee concepts of self and suggest a plan whereby both Indian knowledge and the knowledge and skills needed in school and in the majority society can be developed in the years from preschool through grade twelve. Sternberg (1990)—who deals with styles in terms of the scope and forms of mental self-government—notes the tendency of teachers and schools to reward students whose styles match their own and emphasizes students' need to develop the ability to move from one style to another.

Ausburn and Ausburn advocate assisting learners whose information-processing pattern is not compatible with the task by "planned *supplantation* involving overt alteration of the task requirement." Supplantation will include:

1. Conciliatory supplantation, which capitalizes on the student's preferred method of learning.
2. Compensatory supplantation, which enables learners to compensate for task-related deficiencies by providing for them the process which they themselves cannot yet provide.

(1978:343–44)

They also offer three steps which can be used in lesson design: (1) Task analysis, (2) identification of the students who need supplantation, and (3) planning appropriate conciliatory or compensatory supplantation (1978:344).

3.6 Discussion

In retrospect

The concept of cognitive learning styles has become part of educational theory and is routinely presented in educational texts (e.g., Brown 1980:19–20). The research by Witkin and his colleagues on field dependence-independence has been strongly supported, with some 3,000 references in the literature.

> We have thus far identified a number of cognitive styles. For example: reflectiveness versus impulsiveness (Kagan, Rosman, Day, Albert, and Phillips 1964); cognitive complexity versus simplicity (Bieri 1961); tolerance for unrealistic experiences (Klein, Gardner, and Schlesinger 1962); leveling and sharpening (Gardner, Holzman, Klein, Linton and Spence 1959); serialist holist (Pask 1975); and finally, Witkin's field dependence-independence dimension, which is, by and large, the most extensively investigated cognitive style (Bertini et al. 1986:95).

The research has provided the holistic learner a great service by collecting evidence that a global cognitive style is a bonafide learning style (Cohen 1969:829). This has not always been apparent because of the analytic bias of Western schools. Pask's experimentation has supplied strong evidence that students learn best when taught in their preferred learning style (Domino

1971; Entwistle 1981:95–96). Hansen and Stansfield's recommendations (1982:272) that more research is needed regarding teacher-student match merits more investigation, especially cross-culturally. Kogan's observation (1979, cited by Valencia 1980–81:65) that mathematics is best taught to FD students by an FD teacher also deserves further study.

In support of these scholars the experience of the Summer Institute of Linguistics, an international organization devoted to the study of unwritten languages, can be cited. In Brazil, with competent Brazilian university students, and in England, with high-ranking African university students sent abroad on scholarships, it has been found necessary to develop a global approach for teaching methods of linguistic analysis to holistic learners (Wieseman 1978).

Within the author's family, a holistic linguistics student and a holistic engineering student, both honors pupils, have attested to the frustrations imposed by the use of inductive methods in linguistics and mathematics classrooms. These frustrations have persisted over time, even when the material was understood. Although both holistic and analytic students may learn well with the same methods in second language classes, history, geography and the social sciences, I share Ramirez and Castaneda's (1974:156–57) and Carnine's (1990:377) belief that approaches appropriate for FD students must be developed—at least for the more analytical subjects—if equal educational opportunity is indeed to be provided for all.

Cautions

As regards FD/I theory, however, some cautions are in order. Cox and Ramirez warn that "the concept of cognitive or learning styles of minority and other students is one easily oversimplified and misunderstood or misinterpreted. Unfortunately, it has been used to stereotype minority students or to further label them rather than to identify individual differences that are educationally meaningful" (1981:61).

Malone argues that FD/I testing has been inappropriate for nonliterate traditional communities in which "any manipulation of abstract symbols e.g., embedded figures, is threatening to a people not familiar with this medium." He feels that "the concept of cognitive style requires a deeper exploration of the mythology and characteristic philosophy of life through which cognition is filtered and channeled in traditional societies" (1985:39–41).

Ciborowski and Cole (1971) have identified additional factors—the linguistic influence on the way sensory material is coded for later recall and use, and the extent to which language is involved in the problem-solving process—which also influence concept formation.

As regards molding influences, my experience amongst the ethnolinguistic groups of the Peruvian jungle would not support the theory that parental dominance inevitably produces field dependence (Hansen 1984:313). Field dependence in Peruvian Amazonia tends to be more pronounced in the more permissive societies, while field-independent tendencies are more noticeable among the highly-structured Aguaruna, a culture in which parental responsibilities include strong counselling and disciplinary action.

Reid cautions teachers concerning the "misuse of learning style assessment, diagnosis and prescription" since "the variables that affect learning in general education and in second language learning in particular, are complex" (1987:102). A variety of teaching techniques will be needed.

McKenna (1984), and Widiger, Knudson and Rorer (1980) do not feel that FD/I testing has been conclusive. Widiger et al. state that the results of their testing indicate that "present field dependence-independence measures are best interpreted as ability tests rather than measures of a cognitive style" (1980:116). McKenna reports testing which suggests the evaluative measures used to determine field dependence such as the Embedded Figures Test "do not meet the criteria for a cognitive style at the conceptual level, and at the empirical level there are substantial correlations with standard ability tests" (1984:593). He recommends more testing to assess test-retest reliabilities and convergence among a large variety of cognitive style measures.

McCarty, Lynch, Wallace, and Benally (1991:42–59) cite evidence that questioning format rather than individual learning style is key in concept formation. Open-ended questioning about topics of current interest, freed previously inhibited native American students, normally considered to be global learners, to verbalize and categorize with considerable enthusiasm and skill.

One school of thought entirely rejects Aptitude Treatment Intervention (ATI)—the term used for approaches which accommodate learners' individual differences. Various reasons are cited for this stance, among them research evidence that (1) measures for identifying learning styles are not reliable, (2) relationships between learning-style strengths and academic performance are weak, and (3) instruction matched to students' learning styles had relatively weak effects on academic performance (Carnine 1990:377). A number of educators consider it impractical for a busy teacher to adjust individually to each student. Proponents of this point of view tend to feel that concept formation can be accomplished for everyone with equal effectiveness if instruction is adequate; consequently, teachers need not concern themselves with individual differences. Instead, they should concentrate on including in the lesson all the elements every student needs (elements such as those defined in Gagne's events of learning).

3.7 Conclusion

Despite the limitations of the theories and of the testing, research into cognitive learning styles has furthered our understanding of the preferences and personality differences exhibited by different types of learners in different societies. The core knowledge common to the theories has made us aware of the analytic bias of Western culture, of the intellectual equality of holistic and analytic learners, of influences which mold the development of learning styles, of the need for culturally appropriate methodologies, and of techniques useful for teaching holistic learners. Still, much remains to be known.

The basic research dealing with cognitive learning styles focuses on members of majority cultures. Culturally-sensitive information from minority cultures is relatively sparse. The Australian Departments of Education are conducting research with relation to Aboriginal populations; the findings have broad application in other holistic-type societies. Studies have also been published concerning native North Americans and Spanish speakers in the United States. From developing countries we have some culturally-sensitive anecdotal references, such as those of Bulmer (1983) and Lingenfelter and Gray (1981). The information gleaned has enabled educators to devise methods for teaching holistic learners and also methods for helping students learn to function bicognitively.

As with any movement, cautions and objections have been sounded over the years. One school of thought rejects the concept of individualization of treatment altogether. These objections have certain validity. A teacher's work is increased if treatment is individualized; many learning failures are due to poor quality instruction rather than to learning styles differences; learning styles theory has not always been based on sound empirical evidence, and applications have multiplied to a degree bewildering to many teachers (e.g., Dunn and Dunn 1978; Carbo, Dunn, and Dunn 1986). Nevertheless, the analytic versus global distinction has been supported by much research evidence and appears to be a key factor in many cultures. The weight of our experience points to these two styles, more than any others, as deeply rooted cognitive differences (not merely variance attributable to exposure to Western thinking). They respond best to different treatments, especially in the beginning stages of formal school learning. To overlook these differences results in great frustration for both learners and teachers. Eventually, however, students must be taught to draw upon both styles, suiting the method to the learning task.

At the same time, balance is needed. Not all learning difficulties are attributable to learning style differences, even in cultures where the dichotomy between analytic and holistic learners is salient. An understanding of learning styles is but one tool in the teacher's repertoire; other tools include an understanding of developmental theory and skillful use of information processing theory.

More empirical research is needed from ethnic groups around the world to answer questions such as the following:

1. How are learning styles affected under conditions of culture contact and social change?

2. What molding influences are at work to produce holistic learners in permissive societies?

3. What cross-cultural measures are most effective in helping individuals to appreciate and develop the skills and the strengths of a learning style not their own (i.e., bicognitive performance)?

Studies such as these would not only supply more adequate tools for teachers and educational administrators who work in non-Western societies; they would provide deeper understanding for us all.

References

Albert, Martin L. and Loraine K. Obler. 1978. The bilingual brain: neuropsychological and neurolinguistic aspects of bilingualism. New York: Academic Press.

Ausburn, Lynna J. and Floyd B. Ausburn. 1978. Cognitive styles: some information and implications for instructional design. Education Communication and Technology Journal 26(4):337–54.

Ausubel, David P. 1967. Learning theory and classroom practice. Bulletin No. 1. Toronto: The Ontario Institute for Studies in Education.

————, Joseph D. Novak, and Helen Hanesian. 1978. Educational psychology: a cognitive view. New York: Holt, Rinehart and Winston.

Banks, James A. 1988. Multiethnic education: theory and practice. Boston: Allyn and Bacon.

Baumann, James F. 1984. The effectiveness of a direct instruction paradigm for teaching main idea comprehension. Reading Research Quarterly 20(1):93–115.

Berry, John W. 1966a. Cultural determinants of perception. Ph.D. thesis, University of Edinburgh.

————. 1966b. Temne and Eskimo perceptual skills. International Journal of Psychology 1:207–29.

————. 1976. Human ecology and cognitive style: comparative studies in cultural and psychological adaptation. New York: John Wiley and Sons.

Bertini, Mario. 1986. Some implications of field dependence for education. In Mario Bertini, Luigi Pizzamiglio and Seymour Wapner (eds.), Field dependence in psychological theory, research and application: two symposia in memory of Herman Witkin, 93–106. Hillsdale, New Jersey: Lawrence Erlbaum Associates.

Bieri, J. 1961. Complexity-simplicity as a personality variable in cognitive and preferential behavior. In D. W. Fiske and S. R. Maddi (eds.), Functions of varied experience, 355–79. Homewood, Illinois: Dorsey Press.

Biesheuvel, S. 1949. Psychological tests and their application to non-European peoples. In The yearbook of education, 87–126. London: Evans.

Bowen, Earle and Dorothy Bowen. 1989. Contextualizing teaching methods in Africa. Evangelical Missions Quarterly, July issue.

Brown, H. Douglas. 1980. Principles of language learning and teaching. Englewood Cliffs, New Jersey: Prentice-Hall.

Bruner, J. S., J. J. Goodnow, and G. A. Austin. 1956. A study of thinking. New York: John Wiley and Sons.

Bulmer, Rosalie. 1983. Cultural learning styles: planning a program around local learning styles. Notes on Literacy 39:22–30. Dallas: Summer Institute of Linguistics.

Cahir, Stephen R. 1981. Cognitive styles and the bilingual educator. Bilingual Education Series 10:24–28. Rosslyn, Virginia: National Clearinghouse for Bilingual Education Center for Applied Linguistics.

Carbo, Marie, Rita Dunn, and Kenneth Dunn. 1986. Teaching students to read through their individual learning styles. Englewood Cliffs, New Jersey: Prentice Hall.

Carnine, Douglas. 1990. New research on the brain: implications for instruction. Phi Delta Kappan 71(5):372–77.

Castaneda A. and Tracy Gray. 1974. Bicognitive processes in multicultural education. Educational Leadership 32(3):203–207.

Chapelle, Carol and Cheryl Roberts. 1986. Ambiguity tolerance and field independence as predicators of proficiency in English as a second language. Language Learning 36(1):27–45.

Chrisjohn, R. D. and M. Peters. 1984. The right-brained Indian: fact or fiction? Canadian Journal of Education 13(1):62–71.

Ciborowski, Tom and Michael Cole. 1971. Cultural differences in learning conceptual rules. International Journal of Psychology 6(1):25–37.

Cohen, Rosalie A. 1968. The relation between socio-conceptual styles and orientation to school requirements. Journal of Educational Psychology 41(2):201–220.

————. 1969. Conceptual styles, culture conflict, and nonverbal tests of intelligence. American Anthropologist 71:828–56.

Cox, Barbara G. and Manuel Ramirez III. 1981. Cognitive styles: implications for multiethnic education. In James A. Banks (ed.), Education in the 80's: multiethnic education. Washington, D. C.: National Education Association of the United States.

Crutchfield, R. S., D. G. Woodworth, and R. E. Albrecht. 1958. Perceptual performance and the effective person. Lackland Air Force Base, Texas: Personnel Laboratory, Wright Air Development Center, Air Research and Development Command. ASTIA No. AD-151 039.

Cryns, A. G. J. 1964. African intelligence: a critical survey of cross-cultural intelligence research in Africa south of the Sahara. Journal of Social Psychology 57:283–301.

Das, J. P., J. Manos, and R. N. Kanungo. 1975. Performance of Canadian native, black and white children on some cognitive and personality tests. Alberta Journal of Educational Research 2(3):183–95.

Davis, Patricia M. 1981. The program as it relates to the pupils. In Mildred L. Larson and Patricia M. Davis (eds.), Bilingual education: an experience in Peruvian Amazonia, 227–34. Dallas: Summer Institute of Linguistics and Washington, D. C.: Center for Applied Linguistics.

————. 1987. What we have learned about learning. Notes on Literacy Special Issue 3:1–10. Dallas: Summer Institute of Linguistics.

———— and Martha A. Jakway. 1983. Manual de pedagogia. Yarinacocha, Peru: Ministry of Education and the Summer Institute of Linguistics.

Davis, Thomas and Alfred Pyatskowit. 1976. Bicognitive education: a new future for the Indian child? Journal of American Indian Education 15(3):14–21.

Dawson, J. L. M. 1963. Psychological effects of social change in a West African community. Ph.D. thesis, University of Oxford.

————. 1967. Cultural and physiological influences upon spatial perceptual processes in West Africa. Parts I and II. International Journal of Psychology 2:115–128, 171–85.

Domino, G. 1971. Interactive effects of achievement orientation and teaching style on academic achievement. ACT Research Report 39:1–9.

Doyle, Joseph C., Robert Ornstein, and David Galin. 1974. Lateral specialization of cognitive mode: II. EEG frequency analysis. Psychophysiology 2(5):567–78.

Dunn, Rita. 1988. Teaching students through their perceptual strengths or preferences. Journal of Reading 31(4):304–309.

———— and Kenneth Dunn. 1978. Teaching students through their individual learning styles: a practical approach. Reston, Virginia: Reston Publishing Company.

Edwards, Betty. 1979. Drawing on the right side of the brain. Los Angeles: J. P. Tarcher.

Entwistle, Noel. 1981. Styles of learning and teaching. New York: John Wiley and Sons.

Fadley, J. and V. Hosler. 1979. Understanding the alpha child at home and school: left and right hemispheric function in relation to personality and learning. Springfield, Illinois: Charles C. Thomas.

————. 1983. Case studies in left and right hemispheric functioning. Springfield, Illinois: Charles C. Thomas.

Fitzgibbons, D., L. Goldberger, and M. Eagle. 1965. Field dependence and memory for incidental material. Perceptual and Motor Skills 21:743–49.

Fleming, M. L., J. Q. Knowlton, B. B. Blaine, W. H. Levie, and A. Elerian. 1968. Message design: the temporal dimension of message structure. Final Report. Bloomington, Indiana: Indiana University Press.

Gardner, R., P. Holzman, G. Klein, D. Linton, and D. Spence. 1959. Cognitive control: a study of individual consistencies in cognitive behavior. In Psychological Issues IV. New York: International Press.

Gibson, G. 1950. The perception of the visual world. Cambridge, Massachusetts: Riverside Press.

Goodenough, D. R. 1976. The role of individual differences in field dependence as a factor in learning and memory. Psychological Bulletin 83:675–94.

Graham, Beth. 1980a. Starting where they are: rethinking Aboriginal early childhood education. The Aboriginal Child at School 9(1):28–40.

————. 1980b. Wangkami: a handbook for Aboriginal teachers involved in early childhood education. Darwin, Australia: N. T. Department of Education.

Greene, M. A. 1972. Client perception of the relationship as a function of worker-client cognitive styles. Ph.D. dissertation, Columbia University.

Greenfield, Patricia Marks and Jerome S. Bruner. 1966. Culture and cognitive growth. International Journal of Psychology l(2):89–107.

Guilford, J. P. 1950. Creativity. American Psychologist 5:444–54.

Hansen, Jaqueline and Charles Stansfield. 1982. Student-teacher cognitive styles and foreign language achievement: a preliminary study. Modern Language Journal 66(3):263–73.

Hansen, Lynne. 1984. Field dependence-independence and language testing: evidence from six Pacific island cultures. TESOL Quarterly 18(2):311–34.

Harris, Stephen. 1980. Towards a sociology of Aboriginal literacy. Plenary address of the Sixth Australian Reading Conference, 1–27. Canberra. Files of author.

————. 1982. Traditional Aboriginal education strategies and their possible place in a modern bicultural school. In John Sherwood (ed.), Aboriginal education: issues and innovations. Perspectives in Multicultural Education II, 127–39. Perth: Creative Research.

Hernandez, Hilda. 1989. Multicultural education: a teacher's guide to content and process. Columbus, Ohio: Merrill Publishing Company.

Herold, P. Leslie, Manual Ramirez III, and Alfredo Castaneda. 1974. Field sensitive and field independent teaching strategies. In New approaches to bilingual, bicultural education, 65–76. Austin, Texas: The Dissemination and Assessment Center for Bilingual Education.

Kagan, J., B. L. Rossman, D. Day, J. Albert, and W. Phillips. 1964. Information processing in the child: significance of analytic and reflective attitudes. Psychological Monographs 78:1.

Kauback, Brent. 1984. Styles of learning among native children: a review of the research. Canadian Journal of Native Education 11(3):27–37.

Kaufman, A. S. and N. L. Kaufman. 1983. Kaufman assessment battery for children, interpretive manual. Circle Pines, Minnesota: American Guidance Service.

Kindell, Gloria and Pamela Hollman. To appear. Lesson plan using global teaching strategies. Horsleys Green, England: Summer Institute of Linguistics.

Kinsbourne, M. 1982. Hemisphere specialization and the growth of human understanding. American Psychologist 37:411–20.

Klein, G. C., R. W. Gardner, and H. J. Schlesinger. 1962. Tolerance for unrealistic experiences: a study of the generality of cognitive controls. British Journal of Psychology 53:41–55.

Klich, L. Z. and Graham R. Davidson. 1984. Toward a recognition of Australian Aboriginal competence in cognitive functions. In John R. Kirby (ed.), Cognitive strategies and educational performance, 155–202. Orlando, Florida: Academic Press.

Kogan, Nathan. 1979. Cognitive styles: implications for education. Paper presented at the National Conference on Educational Choices, Omaha, Nebraska.

Kolb, David A. 1984. Experiential learning: experience as the source of learning and development. Englewood Cliffs, New Jersey: Prentice-Hall.

Krashen, Stephen D. 1976. Cerebral asymmetry. In Haiganoosh Whitaker and Harry A. Witaker (eds),. Perspectives in neurolinguistics and psycholinguistics II, 157–91. New York: Academic Press.

Krywanuik, L. L. 1974. Patterns of cognitive abilities of high and low achieving school children. Ph.D. thesis, University of Alberta, Edmonton.

Laosa, Luis M. 1977. Cognitive styles and learning strategies research: some of the areas in which psychology can contribute to personalized instruction in multicultural education. Journal of Teacher Education 28(3):26–30.

Levy, Jerre. 1985. Right brain, left brain: fact and fiction. Psychology Today 5:38–44.

Lewis, D. 1976a. Route finding by desert Aborigines in Australia. Journal of Navigation 29:21–38.

———. 1976b. Observations on route-finding and spatial orientation among the Aboriginal peoples of the western desert region of central Australia. Oceania 46:249–82.

Lingenfelter, Judith and Claire Gray. 1981. The importance of learning styles in literacy. Notes on Literacy 36:11–17. Dallas: Summer Institute of Linguistics.

Luria, A. R. 1966. The human brain and psychological processes. New York: Harper and Row.

MacArthur, R. S. 1968. Some differential abilities of northern Canadian youth. International Journal of Psychology 3(1):43–51.

Malone, Mike. 1985. An analysis of differences in cognitive development in selected African and Western societies. Anthropology and Appropriate Education 31:35–97.

McCarthy, Bernice. 1980. The 4-mat system: teaching to learning styles with right/left mode techniques. Barrington, Illinois: Excel.

McCarty, T. L., Stephen Wallace, Regina Hadley Lynch, and AnCita Benally 1991. Classroom inquiry and Navajo learning styles: a call for reassessment. Anthropology and Education Quarterly 22(1):42–59.

McEachern, William and Verna Kirkness. 1987. Teacher education for Aboriginal groups: one model and suggested application. Journal of Education for Teaching 13(2):133–44.

McKeever, Walter and Michael Dixon. 1981. Right hemisphere superiority for discriminating memorized from non-memorized faces: affective imagery, sex, and perceived emotionality effects. Brain and Language 12:246–60.

McKenna, Frank P. 1984. Measures of field dependence: cognitive style or cognitive ability? Journal of Personality and Social Psychology 47(3):593–603.

Meister Vitale, Barbara. 1985. Unicorns are real: a right-brained approach to learning. Rolling Hills Estates, California: Jalmer Press.

Messick, Samuel. 1978. Personality consistencies in cognition and creativity. In S. Messick and Associates (eds.), Individuality in learning, 4–33. San Francisco: Jossey-Bass Publishers.

More, Arthur J. 1984. Learning styles and Indian students: a review of the research. Paper presented to the Mokakit Indian Education Research Conference, July, London, Ontario.

National Association of Secondary School Principals. 1979. Student learning styles: diagnosing and prescribing programs. Reston, Virginia.

Nebelkopf, E. B. and A. S. Dreyer. 1973. Continuous-discontinuous concept attainment as a function of individual differences in cognitive style. Perceptual and Motor Skills 36:655–62.

Pask, G. 1976a. Conversational techniques in the study and practice of education. British Journal of Educational Psychology 46:12–25.

———. 1976b. Styles and strategies of learning. British Journal of Educational Psychology 46:128–48.

———. 1975. Conversation, cognition and learning: cybernetic theory and methodology. Amsterdam: Elsevier.

——— and B. C. E. Scott. 1972. Learning strategies and individual competence. International Journal of Man-Machine Studies 4:217–53.

Pepper, Floy D. and Steven L. Henry. c. 1984. Excerpts from understanding Indian student behavioral learning styles. Portland, Oregon: Northwest Regional Educational Laboratory.

———. 1984. Social and cultural effects on Indian learning style: classroom implications. Canadian Journal of Native Education 13(1):54–61.

Polich, John M. 1982. Hemispheric differences for visual search: serial vs. parallel processing revisited. Neuropsychologia 20(3):297–307.

Ramirez III, Manual and Alfredo Castaneda. 1974. Cultural democracy, bicognitive development, and education. New York: Academic Press.

Reid, Joan M. 1987. The learning style preferences of ESL students. TESOL Quarterly 21(1):87–111.

Reinert, Harry. 1976. One picture is worth a thousand words? Not necessarily! The Modern Language Journal 60(4):160–68.

Rice, Berkeley. 1979. Brave new world of intelligence testing. Psychology Today 13(4):27–41.

Ruble, D. N. and C. Y. Nakamura. 1972. Task orientation vs. social orientation in young children and their attention to relevant social cues. Child Development 43:471–80.

Schooling, Stephen. 1984. Using culturally appropriate pedagogical methods in training mother-tongue translators. Notes on Translation 100. Dallas: Summer Institute of Linguistics.

———. 1987. Choosing an appropriate teaching style for training mother-tongue translators. Notes on Translation 120. Dallas: Summer Institute of Linguistics.

Seder, J. A. 1957. The origin of differences in extent of independence in children: developmental factors in perceptual field dependence. B.A. thesis, Radcliffe College.

Sodemann, Jean. 1987. Learning styles and their effect on training across cultures. Notes on Translation 120. Dallas: Summer Institute of Linguistics.

Sperry, R. W. 1969. A modified concept of consciousness. Psychological Review 76:532–36.

Springer, Sally and George Deutsch. 1981. Left brain, right brain. San Francisco: W. H. Freeman.

Sternberg, Robert J. 1990. Thinking styles: keys to understanding student performance. Phi Delta Kappan 71(5):366–371.

Swisher, Karen and Donna Deyhle. 1987. Styles of learning and learning styles: educational conflicts for American Indian/Alaskan native youth. Journal of Multilingual and Multicultural Development 8(4):345–60.

Ten Houten, W. D. 1971. Cognitive styles and social order. Final Report, Part II. O.E.O. Study B00-5135, Thought, race and opportunity. Los Angeles: University of California.

Tyler, Leona E. 1965. The psychology of human differences. New York: Appleton-Century Crofts.

Valencia, Atilano A. 1980–81. Cognitive styles and related determinants: a reference for bilingual education teachers. National Association for Bilingual Education Journal 5(2):57–68.

Weinstein, C. F. and R. F. Mayer. 1986. The teaching of learning strategies. In Handbook of research on teaching. New York: McMillan.

Weitz, J. M. 1971. Cultural change and field dependence in two native Canadian linguistic families. Ph.D. dissertation, University of Ottawa.

Widiger, Thomas A, Roger M. Knudson, and Leonard G. Rorer. 1980. Convergent and discriminant validity of measures of cognitive styles and abilities. Journal of Personality and Social Psychology 39(1):116–29.

Williams, Linda Verlee. 1983. Teaching for the two-sided mind. Englewood Cliffs, New Jersey: Simon and Shuster.

Wiseman, Ursula. 1978. Report on Brazil Summer Institute of Linguistics Course. Notes on Linguistics. Dallas: Summer Institute of Linguistics.

Witkin, Herman A. 1967. A cognitive-style approach to cross-cultural research. International Journal of Psychology 2(4):233–50.

———. 1969. Social influences in the development of cognitive style. In David A. Goslin (ed.), Handbook of socialization theory and research, 687–706. Chicago: Rand McNally and Company.

———. 1974. Cognitive styles across cultures. In J. W. Berry and P. R. Dasen (eds.), Culture and cognition: readings in cross-cultural psychology, 99–117. London: Methuen.

————. 1976. Cognitive style in academic performance and in teacher-student relations. In Samuel Messick and Associates (eds.), Individuality in learning, 38–72. San Francisco: Jossey-Bass Publishers.

————. 1978. Cognitive styles in personal and cultural adaptation. Worcester, Massachusetts: Clark University Press.

————, C. A. Moore, D. R. Goodenough, and P. W. Cox. 1977. Field-dependent and field-independent cognitive styles and their educational implications. Review of Educational Research 47(1):1–64.

———— and Donald R. Goodenough. 1981. Cognitive styles. Essence and origins: field dependence and field independence. New York: International Universities Press.

Appendix A
Example of an Advance Organizer:
The Concept of Era[1]

1. Background

For many years I have worked with a bilingual school program designed by the Peruvian Ministry of Education for minority ethnolinguistic groups of the Peruvian jungle. One evening, one of the teacher trainees, a highly intelligent man from one of the more isolated language groups, looked up at me and inquired, "Senora, who came first—Jesus Christ or the Inca?"

2. Preexisting cognitive structure

Amazonia cultures are oral cultures. Their most ancient records are stored in the memories of the grandparents. Time more remote than that is essentially one block, with vague differentiation between remote and very remote past occasionally alluded to in speech or in the legends. I realized immediately that my student's problem was not that he had not read concerning ancient civilizations or heard dates, for he had graduated from high school, but that he had not assembled the conceptual tools necessary to deal with ancient eras of time. Even though he had learned to number years—1982, 1983, 1984, etc.—I suspected that he did not relate those numbers to the distant past or understand their origin.

I managed an explanation which so enthralled the student and all his friends within earshot, that they asked questions for two hours; but if I had

---

[1]This example is more complex than many advance organizers need to be, but it will serve to illustrate the method of presentation.

known what I now know, I could have begun my explanation with a comparative Advance Organizer, as follows.

3. Behavioral objective

At the end of this Advance Organizer, the student will be able to (a) diagram two eras on a time line, and (b) explain the following with one hundred percent accuracy.

(1) Time is divided into large blocks, called eras.

(2) Eras are often named for the people who had controlling power.

(3) An era covers many lifetimes.

(4) Some eras are longer than others.

4. The Advance Organizer (comparative type)

Think of time as a line which begins so far back that no one can remember when it started and which will continue in the future for longer than we can imagine, like this:

We can represent ourselves on the line:

Before us, came our parents:

Before our parents, came our grandparents and great-grandparents:

And there were ancestors before that:

When your people talk, they speak of "your father's time" or "when your grandfather was alive." The written history that we have from other lands, however, covers many more years and the lifetimes of so many people that we must make larger divisions than just the lifetimes of the ancestors whom we can remember. For this reason, people began to divide history into large blocks. Each block is called a *period* or an *era*, and we often give an era the name of the people who were in control during that period.

For example, we could divide the history of the jungle into two large eras:

Era 1   Era 2

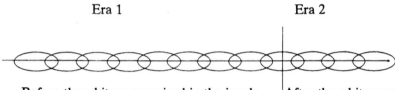

Before the white man arrived in the jungle.   After the white man arrived in the jungle

Your ancestors did not count years, but now that you do, you can tell that eras are sometimes long, and sometimes short. The era before the coming of the white man to the jungle, for example, was much longer than the era since his coming.

5. The Advance Organizer as a concept

This Advance Organizer begins with the student's very limited knowledge of history by reminding him of the passing of time and the sequencing of the generations of his family. It continues to draw on his knowledge, pointing out that the lives of people fall within much larger time divisions.

Thus far, I have merely been organizing the student's knowledge. Now new information is added: The name *era* is attached to large time divisions. This label is a new vocabulary item, but it also functions as a new concept because it identifies as a separate entity an idea which previously was vague and unfocused. The vocabulary item has to be learned by rote, but the concept is learned by correlative subsumption, since it is merely an extension of previous knowledge.

The new concept *era* will include all the time divisions historians (or anyone else) care to define. Those presented in the lesson, therefore, will be learned by analogy and derivative subsumption.

Sequencing of eras, labeling of eras, and variable time length of eras are all aspects included in the concept as soon as there is more than one era and it becomes necessary to distinguish between them. Once the student has been alerted to these possibilities in the advance organizer, he will understand their occurrence in the lesson through analogy and derivative subsumption.

Since the student has been alerted to the fact that years and eras are related, it is possible to teach the system used for the numbering of years through extension of information and correlative subsumption.

The common features which run throughout the advance organizer and the lesson are: the passing of time, division of time into eras, labeling of eras, measuring of time, and the subdivision of eras into generations.

This Advance Organizer excludes other ways of looking at history, such as the sequence of major inventions, the development of writing systems, the diffusion of languages, and the spread of colonialism.

6. Content to be taught

We have written historical records for some 4,000 to 5,000 years, but only from certain parts of the world. What we know, we can chart in large eras, according to the people who held control, just as we did when we charted the time before and after the white man came to the jungle. Some of the important divisions found in history books are the following (information taken from the Encyclopedia Britannica):

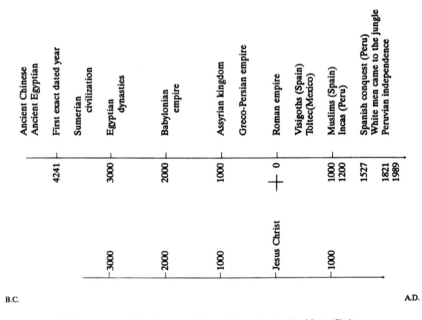

Years are counted backwards and forwards from the death of Jesus Christ.

7. Conclusion

Now you know some of the important eras of history:

- You know some of the peoples who had controlling power;
- You know the order in which these eras occurred;
- You know how we count years; and
- You know that Jesus Christ came before the Inca.

Figure 1. Preexisting cognitive structure
(Dotted lines indicate relationships which are vague and not clearly defined.)

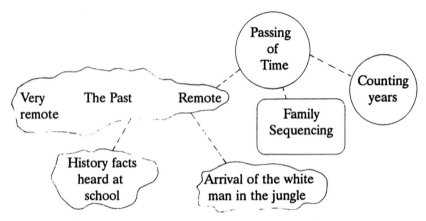

Figure 2. Cognitive structure after the advance organizer

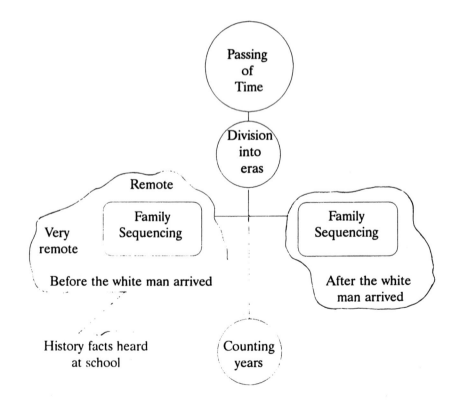

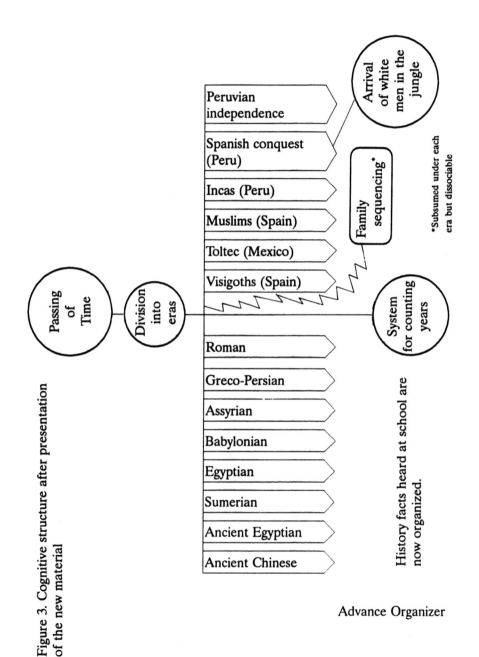

Figure 3. Cognitive structure after presentation of the new material

Advance Organizer

Appendix B
Checklist for Effective Cross-cultural Teacher Training

1. Have at least two Aboriginal teachers in the group; three or four is ideal. If you work with only one Aboriginal teacher, invite someone else to join the group. In time, aim to involve some parents in discussion sessions.

2. Timetable teacher development sessions or dialogues; do not leave them to chance. You will probably need about three each week.

3. Allow at least half an hour for each session; the end of the day is not always the best time.

4. Find a place where the Aboriginal teachers are comfortable. Sitting on the floor or under a shady tree may be best. A cup of tea or a cold drink can often help to create the relaxed atmosphere that you require.

5. Plan a common experience to introduce dialogue. Draw the learning of the group from this common meeting place.

6. Do not leave a topic until you have worked out how to implement the ideas you have been discussing. This will often involve making or collecting appropriate materials, making games or story books, or developing some program outlines.

7. Avoid using educational 'jargon' unless it is explained and frequently reinforced.

8. Allow time for the Aboriginal teachers to talk things over together in their own language and then tell you what they have talked about.

9. 'Hasten slowly' is the rule. Don't attempt too much too quickly.

10. Let teachers illustrate information if listing proves to be difficult.

11. Translating educational ideas into the vernacular is a slow process. Allow time for understanding and check with others such as the local linguist or more experienced staff.

12. Let content suggestions develop from an understanding of theory. Good theory will lead to good practice.

13. Carry understandings learned at teacher training sessions into program planning times.

14. Share the leadership if at all possible, making use of more experienced Aboriginal teachers or those with some training.

15. If you have asked someone else to lead do not take over and do it for them. If you feel you are going to interfere, go away and leave them to it. They can report back later.

16. Do not be afraid of silence—learn to relax and wait for others to talk. If necessary, rephrase the question but do not supply the answer. If there is still no response from the group, suggest they talk about it in their own language because maybe they have not understood the question and need to clarify it.

17. Remember that Aboriginal people use a lot of nonverbal language when they are communicating. Learn to 'hear' this also.

18. Learn to listen not just to the words people say but to the ideas they are trying to convey. (Remember that expressing ideas in a second language is difficult.)

19. Remember people learn more from the things they think out for themselves than they do from the things they are told.

(Graham 1980a:28–40)

CPSIA information can be obtained at www.ICGtesting.com
Printed in the USA
LVOW122306010513

331853LV00016B/279/P